Ethics for Peacebuilders

ABOUT THE PEACE AND SECURITY IN THE 21ST CENTURY SERIES

Until recently, security was defined mostly in geopolitical terms with the assumption that it could only be achieved through at least the threat of military force. Today, however, people from as different backgrounds as planners in the Pentagon and veteran peace activists think in terms of human or global security, where no one is secure unless everyone is secure in all areas of their lives. This means that it is impossible nowadays to separate issues of war and peace, the environment, sustainability, identity, global health, and the like.

The books in the series aim to make sense of this changing world of peace and security by investigating security issues and peace efforts that involve cooperation at several levels. By looking at how security and peace interrelate at various stages of conflict, the series explores new ideas for a fast changing world and seeks to redefine and rethink what peace and security mean in the first decades of the new century.

Multidisciplinary in approach and authorship, the books cover a variety of topics, focusing on the overarching theme that students, scholars, practitioners, and policymakers have to find new models and theories to account for, diagnose, and respond to the difficulties of a more complex world. Authors are established scholars and practitioners in their fields of expertise.

In addition, it is hoped that the series will contribute to bringing together authors and readers in concrete, applied projects, and thus help create, under the sponsorship of Alliance for Peacebuilding (AfP), a community of practice.

The series is sponsored by the Alliance for Peacebuilding, http://www.allianceforpeacebuilding.org/ and edited by Charles Hauss, government liaison.

Ethics for Peacebuilders

A Practical Guide

Reina C. Neufeldt

ROWMAN & LITTLEFIELD
Lanham • Boulder • New York • London

Published by Rowman & Littlefield
A wholly owned subsidiary of The Rowman & Littlefield Publishing Group, Inc.
4501 Forbes Boulevard, Suite 200, Lanham, Maryland 20706
www.rowman.com

Unit A, Whitacre Mews, 26-34 Stannary Street, London SE11 4AB

British Library Cataloguing in Publication Information Available

Library of Congress Cataloging-in-Publication Data

Names: Neufeldt, Reina C., author.
Title: Ethics for peacebuilders : a practical guide / Reina C. Neufeldt.
Description: Lanham : Rowman & Littlefield, [2016] | Series: Peace and security in the 21st century series | Includes bibliographical references and index.
Identifiers: LCCN 2016013413 (print) | LCCN 2016024769 (ebook) | ISBN 9781442264915 (cloth : alk. paper) | ISBN 9781442264922 (pbk. : alk. paper) | ISBN 9781442264939 (Electronic)
Subjects: LCSH: Peace-building—Moral and ethical aspects. | Peace—Moral and ethical aspects.
Classification: LCC JZ5581 .N48 2016 (print) | LCC JZ5581 (ebook) | DDC 172/.42--dc23
LC record available at https://lccn.loc.gov/2016013413

™ The paper used in this publication meets the minimum requirements of American National Standard for Information Sciences—Permanence of Paper for Printed Library Materials, ANSI/NISO Z39.48-1992.

Printed in the United States of America

Contents

Figures, Tables, and Textboxes

LIST OF FIGURES

LIST OF TABLES

LIST OF TEXTBOXES

Preface

"If you run at the mouth, your feet may not catch up."

This book project came about through reflections on my work as a peacebuilder, and in an effort to come to terms with some of the challenges I encountered supporting peacebuilding work with grassroots and civil society groups and organizations. There were constantly events and questions that invoked moral values for which I was ill-equipped to respond—some of which are further detailed in the chapters that follow.

"Your views of peacebuilding are limited. You think all people have agency. That they are equally capable of making changes," the priest said. It was 2002, and his argument was that we were not paying enough attention to economic and political structures.

"Why are you people so committed to nonviolence?" my Serbian colleague exhorted. Such a dogmatic commitment was blinding he insisted.

"Changing customs is the hardest thing," my Kenyan colleague exclaimed. She was speaking about the challenges of changing female rites of passage. "No, changing people is the hardest thing," my Rwandan colleague responded. "You never know what is going on inside someone's head. You can never access it."

It took some years, but I slowly came to realize the importance of moral values in shaping our discourse about, and choices in, peacebuilding. These quotations, which are my approximations of what my colleagues said at the time (as I didn't record them), pointed to value assumptions that were being questioned with respect to what was the good end that peacebuilding pursued, or what was judged the right thing to do. The priest was intoning that it was not good enough peacebuilding if we only addressed schisms in social relationships without attending to the gross structural inequities in settings of deep rooted conflict. My Serbian colleague—who had experienced dogmatisms run amok—was arguing that any moral value commitment not thoroughly questioned was dogmatic and a potential problem. My Kenyan and Rwandan colleagues were articulating that they each saw different ends as not only being the hardest but also the most important. Individual change was not only profoundly difficult to access and assess, it was also of great import if it was achieved, my Rwandan colleague was saying. Likewise, my Kenyan colleague thought that changing a deep-rooted and problematic cultural norm was both difficult and of great worth.

Even as I became aware of the values dimension of our conversations, I struggled mightily with the idea of writing a book on peacebuilding ethics. Not with the idea that doing or being good is important—that I had plenty of from growing up with Mennonite pacifist faith convictions. What I struggled with was the idea that ethics offered an answer; that by writing a book on ethics, I would be expected to provide an answer. This was not at all what I aimed to produce. I was (and am) well aware that I did (do) not have all of the answers and was limited in my ability to speak to what the right thing to do was. In the end, this book is about ethics as a process of asking better questions about peacebuilding values, listening for values, and the ways in which values inform our work. My hope is that it will help open up space for talking about values, reflecting and responding to values more carefully in the midst of peacebuilding work in an effort to make it better—which I recognize will be defined in different ways by different people.

The photograph on the front of the book was taken by Dave Klassen. It captures a part of the city of Jos, in Plateau State, Nigeria, that was hit hard by violence in 2010. I was standing nearby when Dave took the photo, as part of a learning trip, and provided some minor technical support to Mennonite Central Committee's efforts to work with local grassroots peacebuilders. For me, this image captures many of the challenges of working in and on peacebuilding: there is destruction and regrowth, crumbling walls and branches reaching into the sky, sharp barbed wire and new life encircling it. Loss and hope, fear and courage, quiet and vibrancy all around. It is in these types of contexts that we engage, based upon our beliefs of what is important, what is valued, and what is good, and in which we can do great harm. By bringing discussions of moral values and ethics into the picture, my hope is that we will gain further clarity, be better peacebuilders, and our peacebuilding will be the better for it.

There are many people who have contributed to my thinking about values, peacebuilding, and ethics to whom I am very grateful. First and foremost, thanks to the many peacebuilders with whom I have been privileged to work and learn—they are too many to name, but include among others Liliana Amaral, Tom Bamat, Emmanuel Bombande, Jaco Cilliers, Deng Giguiento, Susan Hahn, William Headley, John Paul Lederach, Myla Leguro, Chea Muoy Kry, Adriano do Nascimento, Grace Ndugu, Paul Rutayisire, Alex Schein, Brian Starken, Jean-Baptiste Talla, and Philip Visser. Thanks to Todd Whitmore for conversations about ethics and peacebuilding, and encouraging me to take a closer look at virtue ethics back in 2007. Thanks to Ron Fisher for encouraging me to teach a course on the topic of ethics and peacebuilding at American University, and for Conrad Grebel University College for supporting a new version of the course and providing me with time to write. Thanks also to the students who have taken the various iterations of the course, and who have offered-up their sharp insights and enthusiasm in exploring moral issues. Further thanks to the various guest speakers in the class who shared moral dilemmas and analysis, including Michael Barnett, Chuck Call, Joe Eldridge, Frances Fortune, Mary Lou Klassen, George Lopez, Mvuselelo Ngcoya, Joji and Dan Pantoja, Rami Shamma, and Krista Johnson Weicksel.

My appreciation also goes to those who provided feedback on the manuscript and helped shape it into a better document. All errors and shortcomings remain mine. Mary Anderson and Mark Rogers read an early version of the manuscript and provided helpful feedback. Howard Zehr and Lisa Schirch suggested there was life in the project when I was not so sure. Aldred Neufeldt and Narendran Kumarakulasingam read the revised manuscript in full and provided thoughtful comments. Thanks to Chip Hauss and Marie-Claire Antoine for their support and including the book in the Alliance for Peacebuilding and Rowman & Littlefield joint series. Finally, thanks to Naren for accompanying me on a life journey, and consistently helping me discover what it means to be moral in this world.

1

Doing Good?

"I am looking to get my soul back," the young woman said. She had recently left Afghanistan after a number of years working on peacebuilding and reconstruction work, including some time working as a civilian assisting Provincial Reconstruction Teams (PRTs).[1] *Her story was similar to many others who engage in humanitarian and peacebuilding work—myself included—although her experiences were, in many ways, extreme. She began working in peacebuilding and development assistance to make a difference, to do good things, to help people. She went to Afghanistan because the needs were great. There were calls for assistance, particularly working on participatory development projects.*

After some years of working with local, non-governmental organizations and feeling like there was little impact from their work, she decided the work would have greater effect if she moved to a larger organization, which involved engaging with PRTs and the International Security Assistance Force (ISAF). ISAF was initially established by the United Nations Security Council in 2001 to assist the Afghan Interim Authority "in the maintenance of security in Kabul and its surrounding areas" (S/Res/1386),[2] *and was led by the North Atlantic Treaty Organization (NATO). PRTs were developed in 2002 to provide security, assess needs, and assist with humanitarian response or small-scale reconstruction tasks. These were teams of fifty to 150 people, run by different NATO member countries, comprised primarily of military personnel with a handful of civilians who were included for their respective areas of technical expertise. While working with the PRTs, the young woman had faced violence, and was indirectly implicated in the loss of life. Well-intentioned aid had gone wrong when some resources distributed after an earthquake were turned into improvised explosive devices that had killed some friends. How could she live with this knowledge, she wondered, and how could she still trust people when she (and others) felt terribly betrayed on this and other occasions? Yet there were also moments that seemed good in this work, where important services had been restored, and there were moments of connection and rapport with women in rural areas. Were these illusions?*

The experiences in this opening vignette get to the core of why most of us do peacebuilding work—because we want to do *good*, we want to contribute to life, to justice, to flourishing. And, the experiences lay bare the reality that things happen, *bad* things happen, even when we aim to help people. Sometimes the bad things are clear, as when people's lives are lost as a direct or indirect result of our actions. Many times, however, the bad things are less clear, such as when we contribute to projects that divert resources, send subtle messages about the inferiority of local ways of doing things, or suggest interventions that poorly match with what the local community wants or needs. In these cases we might discover we were wrong years later when we find, for example, that our work made no difference, or work we did to empower one group generated painful new rifts and even was a factor in retaliatory violence in the community. While less obvious, contributing to social or economic divisions can have very long-lasting negative effects.[3]

The experiences in the opening vignette also speak to the importance of the decisions that we make along the way. The little decisions and choices that we make in response to practical challenges—like what kind of material aid to distribute or whom to partner with—actually have moral dimensions and present moral challenges. We may regret our decisions months and years later when the material aid gets used to harm others. Choices like whom to work for and how to influence change are also decisions with moral dimensions; they are based upon particular moral values that we hold. We choose to work for organizations which emphasize participatory processes over speed in interventions, or for organizations that value scale over participatory processes (see discussion in chapter 6). We may also discover that people and communities hold divergent moral values, or perhaps hold the same values but feel they have been treated unjustly and so how those values are understood and expressed then diverge. Whether similar or different, obvious or hidden, moral values play a role in the practical choices we make.

Hannah Arendt once noted, "The sad truth of the matter is that most evil is done by people who never made up their mind to be either bad or good" (1971, p. 438). Arendt was trying to make sense of Adolf Eichmann's "curious, quite authentic *inability to think*" [emphasis added] (p. 417), particularly in moral terms when on trial for his Nazi–era crimes in Jerusalem. We can the moral dimensions of our work; and, to confront the moral challenges that we face in life-giving ways.

PEACEBUILDING'S GOOD INTENTIONS

For this book, peacebuilding is defined broadly and refers to efforts undertaken before, during, or after violent conflict which focus not only on stopping violence, but also address and transform the deeply-rooted structural issues and divisive social relationships that drive conflict.[4] Peacebuilding therefore aims to achieve a sustainable and just peace in conflict-affected communities. This definition is similar to Johan Galtung's inaugural definition of the term in the 1970s, which distinguished efforts aimed at keeping peace or making peace (stopping conflict and negotiating solutions to problems) from the relational and structural elements of peace work. Notice the moral values already apparent in this definition—the valuing of social relationships, of sustainability, and of justice. These are "moral goods" that are directly connected to how peacebuilding is practiced.

There are other definitions of peacebuilding that may more narrowly constrain or broadly expand the values of peacebuilding. For example, definitions that focus on preventing the recurrence of violence only foreground the value of human life, and do not include judgments about the quality of that life when it is lived. Other definitions suggest ends, such as the definition that guides this book. Some definitions are even more specific, and name particular peacebuilding ends like building stable democratic institutions—here a particular political system is valued as a good end in and of itself. Additional values articulated by stakeholders involved in civil society peacebuilding interventions often include nonviolent and participatory means.

The differences in basic definitions of peacebuilding provide us with a starting point for understanding the values we hold in peacebuilding, and point to differences in values. At times, these values are in tension, such as when a focus on the good of stability is contrasted with an emphasis on participatory processes. When we experience tension, it is a helpful starting point for us to take notice of values, as will be explored further in chapter 3.

Tensions in moral values at times map onto a tension between "top-down" and "bottom-up" approaches to peacebuilding. The opening vignette in this chapter features a story that is part of what is often called "top-down" peacebuilding, and connected to the valuing of stability—regional or international stability—as a moral good. Such peacebuilding is driven by top-level political and military leadership, and focuses on various aspects of building or rebuilding state infrastructure in conflict-affected countries, including rule of law programs, economic stability, good governance, and so forth.

The rise in international peacebuilding came with the United Nations' (UN) commitment to more robust engagement on peace-related matters in the 1990s, and was initially articulated in 1992 by then Secretary General Boutros Boutros-Ghali in "An Agenda for Peace." Peacebuilding was officially named as part of the international community's options in assisting countries emerging from conflict, and has developed into its own area of focus in the UN with the formation of the UN Peacebuilding Commission and Peacebuilding Fund. This type of peacebuilding involves large-scale, international efforts, it typically involves outsiders—whether United Nations peacekeepers, peacebuilders, or sector-specific experts—coming into a conflict-affected area to provide particular technical expertise and inputs as part of a state-building project. This approach is often critiqued by and in tension with local-level or "bottom-up" peacebuilding.

"Bottom-up" peacebuilding involves informally or formally organized, local actors engaged in efforts to address the roots of conflict and restore relationships. Its origins, in many ways, pre-date state-level peacebuilding, emerging from and in community-based conflict resolution and conflict transformation efforts. While such efforts have long existed, it wasn't until the 1980s that attention to these activities solidified along with the field of peace and conflict studies. Grassroots peacebuilding initiatives grew and proliferated in the 1990s alongside attention to state-level peacebuilding. Here peacebuilding initiatives are understood to be designed by and led by local actors working within their own setting, which therefore foregrounds the intimate nature of the conflict as well as the valuing of participatory processes. In this type of peacebuilding, if outsiders are involved, they are in the background playing a supportive role, and the focus tends to be a more localized community.

People engage in top-down as well as bottom-up peacebuilding with ideas about the good and the right in mind. We want to change things to how they *ought* to be. This is the same whether we work within our own conflict contexts or we are an outsider working in another's conflict context. Yet, the different values we hold may have blind spots or produce harms when tied to our actions. There are problematic aspects to and moral challenges involved in all types and levels of peacebuilding.

The definition of peacebuilding used for this book signals the kinds of values I hold. However, these values and norms are not uniformly held across the peacebuilding community nor in the communities in which peacebuilding occurs. What follows then is an examination of *how* to think about moral values and ethics, rather than a prescription of what to think. We do not all agree on what is good and right and how a peaceful society should be structured and function, which is important to recognize and validate. We also know that our good intentions do not equal good outcomes or flourishing. Yet, often times, peacebuilders have fallen back on assuming we are doing good work because we have good values and intentions (as our opening vignette reminds us), or we have assumed we are doing good work because we focused on good ends.

Sometimes we may find ourselves blind to the values we bring, particularly when the people around us seem to agree with us on what is good and right. Being blind to one's values is dangerous in conflict zones where value differences are frequently part of the divide. It's also dangerous when we're working on tasks that might involve values imposition, such as can occur in stabilization, economic development, nonviolent social change, democracy, or other types of projects and initiatives. Strong critiques in the literature warn peacebuilders against inadvertently being part of a new era of colonialism (for suggested reading see the Notes section). Such warnings are particularly important because peacebuilding, since the 1990s, has involved outsiders working in other people's moral communities, often with the support of the international community and under United Nations auspices; in these contexts, international peacebuilders can easily be out of tune with the local moral community. Further, moral communities themselves are often frayed and altered by the conflict.

Ethical thinking and action, then, necessarily begins with ourselves and our approach to peacebuilding, creating the space to think about and question our values explicitly. It involves us—as individuals, groups, or organizations—thinking about what and why some things are right or wrong, where these values come from, and how our own views of what is right and wrong, good and bad, just and unjust align or don't align. In short, we need to rethink ethics in practice, and include discussions not only about our means of operating but also our very understanding of effectiveness (see textbox 1.1).

TEXTBOX 1.1.
ETHICS ARE NICE BUT I'M FOCUSED ON EFFECTIVENESS

A common question asked of peacebuilders is "are you being effective?" This question—which has come to dominate funder discussions when deciding what peacebuilding initiatives to support—is driven by a focus on achieving positive outcomes and impacts. This focus raises good questions about what is or will be done, and to what effect, in order to gauge whether or not it is the right thing to do. This focus makes an ethical claim, which is that what is good and right to focus on is the ends of our work defined as effectiveness (see the discussion in chapter

(continued)

4 on consequentialism). Yet, intriguingly, effectiveness is not seen as directly relevant to discussions of ethics—perhaps because the empirical data generated for findings are assumed to provide information on performance that is unrelated to values.

Ethics in practice, it seems, refers to the way we do things and the principles that guide us as individuals and organizations. We have bifurcated or separated the domains of effectiveness and morality. In some areas we consider ethics relevant and appropriate and in other areas ethics considerations are not considered relevant. The report "Confronting War: Critical Lessons for Peace Practitioners" provides a great example of this bifurcation where the term ethics refers to means, and effectiveness involves considerations of ends for which the term ethics does not apply. "Confronting War," written by Mary B. Anderson and Lara Olson in 2003, is a landmark document in the field of peacebuilding because it presents learnings from a large set of case studies regarding what is effective in peace work. It seeks to answer the great, ethically imbued question: *Why isn't all the well-intentioned peace work we are doing adding up to more?* I was fortunate to coauthor a case study used in the collaborative learning process, as well as be involved in consultations that produced the patterns of findings reported in the monograph on what makes for effective peace practice. These findings have been used widely in the field to design and assess peace practice.

For our purposes, it is important to note where ethics is talked about by Anderson and Olson and how it is distinguished from effectiveness. Ethics are specifically named in a short section called "Walking the Walk: How Means Affect Ends in Peace Practice" (pp. 27–34), where the connection between modeling and the means of our practice is discussed in terms of how it affects outcomes. Six dimensions or principles are explored, such as honesty and the valuing of life in peace practice. Most of the rest of the ninety-odd page report focuses on the importance of effects, criteria to assess the effectiveness of peace work, harms to avoid, and strategies to improve the effectiveness of peace practice—these sections do not explicitly mention ethics. It isn't that ethics are unimportant—they are important and discussed in the report—but they are limited and exclude discussions of effectiveness.

This creates a false dichotomy and an unintentional effect is that we limit our considerations of ethics to only one part of work, and perhaps even to only one group (such as grassroots peacebuilders). Ethical considerations of what is morally right and good are actually relevant to both halves of this dichotomy: means *and* ends. Viewing all our claims, including effectiveness, as involving moral value choices opens up a space for conversation about what matters most in our work. This provide us with an opportunity to name and address points of disconnect or disagreement in new ways, and can address tensions such as those that manifest themselves around project evaluation or between top-down and bottom-up peacebuilders.

In the following three sections, we explore some basic tasks for ethical thinking. These three tasks are a starting point for nurturing open and careful thinking. The purpose of the full book is to further support and hone our thinking and communication capacities with respect to ethics in our work as peacebuilders, individually and as members of teams and communities. We will start, however, with foundational tasks to support ethical thinking.

ETHICAL THINKING TASK 1: ASKING QUESTIONS BEFORE PRODUCING ANSWERS

When people think of ethics they are often looking for the right answer—the correct answer that is superior in logic and form to all other possible answers. This is a high ideal, and often not necessary or practical. It is also an approach that many people shy away from because they do not want to get into a detailed argument about what is right, and why it is right. For our purposes, this approach to thinking about ethics is counterproductive because it shuts down alternative possibilities.

In this book, I approach ethics from a pragmatic, applied perspective and start with a focus on questions rather than answers. I also presume that there is no singular right answer. Our purpose is to develop better skills and capacities to identify, weigh, and act upon moral values on a routine basis, to enhance ethical thinking that informs action. Questions, and being able to ask good questions that probe dimensions of the context as well as dimensions of good and right, are therefore where we start in order to make better-informed judgments.

Consider the following scenario, which compiles several experiences into one example:

A peacebuilder working internationally was asked by a local partner to take the lead in a community mediation process. The partner said it would be more impactful if a foreign expert led the process; people would listen more. The funding non-governmental organization was also pressing the peacebuilder for results that it could report to its donors. The peacebuilder was flattered by the partner's request and thought it suggested that after two years of living in this area, she had gained the partner's respect. She also saw the mediation as critical for improving the security in the community, which would have widespread positive effects. She had a suspicion, however, that the request from the partner suggested deep misgivings about the entire mediation process and was "face-saving"; that is, the partner thought it inappropriate but did not want to say so verbally.

Our tendency is to simply respond to such invitations based on our assumptions of what is going on, but gaining better knowledge before deciding will generate better choices. This means we have to ask: What else do we need to know to make sense of this situation in order to understand the rightness or wrongness of our choices more fully? In this scenario, the peacebuilder appears to assume that a successful mediation will produce the greatest good in terms of positive outcomes. That said, the misgivings suggest she holds another value around respecting local practices or a concern about harmful effects.

As readers of the scenario we will have a series of questions. We'll want to know about the quality of the relationship between the international and local partner, the ways in which power plays out in that relationship, the value of authority figures locally, whether or not there is equity, or whether or not the peacebuilder and partner listen and respond to each other's needs well. We might also look for more information about the purpose of the mediation itself, as well as its suitability as a form of intervention. The reference to the donor looking for results also produces questions, such as who is the donor? For what types of results are they looking? For what purpose? What type of values are emphasized when looking for results and how does that compare with the values that the community holds? Asking these types of questions will draw out information that can deepen and improve the deliberations about how to respond ethically and subsequent decisions and actions.

Information that comes in response to our questions can radically shift how we think about the presenting moral issues. For example, perhaps we found out that the donor referred to in the scenario is a community cooperative that is funding the mediation initiative in their own community. This suggests, then, that the funder *is* the community and its values are represented in the types of results it is expecting. This information makes the relationship between our international peacebuilder and the community more fully accountable to the community. This arrangement is very different than if the funder referred to is a foreign government that is assisting the local nongovernmental organization in order to achieve results that feed into its foreign policy aims around local stability. In this second case, we may have strong concerns that we are in danger of external values being imposed upon the community by the outsider. The information we find out about the funder can dramatically shift how we think about their role, the values they bring, and the role those values ought to play in our decision-making. Asking questions before we produce answers is therefore our first task.

ETHICAL THINKING TASK 2: AVOIDING MENTAL SHORTCUTS

A second task for us is to not fall into common traps common in ethical thinking, or rather, we need to avoid ways of thinking that cut short genuine ethical deliberation. American philosopher and teacher Anthony Weston talks about three common substitutes or counterfeits for ethical thinking: dogmatism, relativism, and rationalization (see the Notes section for Weston's books). To think ethically we need to avoid all three of these mental shortcuts.

Dogmatists already know the answer to a moral question before it is raised. They cut off open and careful consideration because they have concluded they know what is right, regardless of the specific case or circumstances. For example, in the United States the debate about abortion is highly acrimonious and frequently led by dogmatists who are willing to take extreme actions because they believe they are morally right. We also have dogmatists in our field of peacebuilding, including those who are so committed to nonviolence that they do not engage with difficult counter-arguments about the use of force, or those who are so committed to the use of force to stop violence that they do not engage with difficult counter-arguments about the use of nonviolent methods to stop violence. Sometimes we agree with the values that dogmatists hold and so we think they are doing good, and at other times we disagree and think they are upholding positions that cannot be sustained morally. In both cases, if we cling to our values without careful and open-ended thinking we risk becoming dogmatists and giving answers before grasping the questions. We need to begin by challenging our assumptions about which values are right, and think about multiple values.[5]

Relativists often dodge moral debate by saying things like "everything is relative" or "to each his own." There is frequently a presumption behind this sentiment that we will all get along if we are easygoing and don't mind others and don't speak up about our values. Interestingly, this approach presumes that all values can coexist, and that this will happen automatically. Yet often conflicts over values do occur, and conflicts can fester over time if not carefully explored. For example, value differences between members of a peacebuilding team will persist and affect work and collaboration over time if some members of the team are solely outcomes focused and others are solely focused on participatory processes. Rather than sweeping divergent values under the rug, we can raise up the values and have open discussions about what values matter for our work, and how we can uphold them together—even if they are conflicting values. Optimal agreements in negotiation come after exploring the diverging needs and interests of both sides, not before. This same finding is applicable for our thinking about ethics in practice: we will come to a deeper understanding of our values and areas of commonality after exploring divergent values rather than before we even mention them.[6]

The third shortcut, rationalization, refers to the tendency to justify our response without thinking too deeply about the issues at hand. When we rationalize we simply provide a one-sided defense of the reasons why we did the right thing. For example, perhaps in response to the intermediary dilemma noted above regarding the request to mediate as an international, we might quickly reject the request and say, "Of course not! I would never lead a mediation that a local organization could lead!" and refuse to be a mediator in this case. This might be ethical, but if we justified this choice by simply saying we were doing our duty and upholding the principle of subsidiarity or enacting good partnership principles then we are rationalizing. For ethical deliberation, we need to consider the values at stake more closely. Which values matter here: Is it the values of our professional conduct? Is it stakeholder participation? Is it outputs? Is it our reputation? Are there multiple values at stake? We also need to consider the intended and unintended effects of our action. If the violence escalated and this escalation was an immediate response to our refusal to mediate then how does that affect what is ethical in this situation? Our decision will be more nuanced and often more creative when we engage in fulsome ethical deliberation and avoid simple justifications.

ETHICAL THINKING TASK 3: CAREFUL LISTENING AND THINKING

At its core, ethical thinking involves open and careful thinking. It is about asking deep and probing questions that surface and weigh the values at stake in a given decision and course of action. This requires a willingness to listen after we ask questions, in order to discover the depth of issues, to probe complexity and find out as much as we can in order to develop informed opinions and judgments. We have to be attentive to values, be open and willing to challenge and change our own ideas in the process, and be self-aware of what we are doing and why. We also need to be prepared to respect others and their views—this too is another form of careful listening. When we find values conflict, then we can move into creative problem-solving that can enrich our thinking.

These three initial tasks to nurture our ways of thinking about ethics are summarized in textbox 1.2. Interestingly, this list is very similar to the list of things that people expect of those who engage in dialogue and mediation in the field of conflict resolution and peacebuilding! We are simply using these skills to explore an underappreciated aspect of our own applied work.

TEXTBOX 1.2. NURTURING ETHICAL THINKING

1. Ask questions before giving answers:
   To draw out diverse points of view and make more informed judgments.
2. Avoid mental shortcuts:
   To stimulate careful thinking, and help us be self-aware of how we think about ethics.
3. Careful listening and thinking:
   To be open to diverse points of view, identify values, respect and respond to others, and provide a base for creative problem-solving when values conflict.

MOVING FORWARD

The challenge for most peacebuilders is to engage with ethics purposefully in order to ensure that we are really living out the values that we want to live out in our work, and are making deliberate choices that consider harms, intentions, and ways of being. The following chapters of this book are dedicated to helping peacebuilders think through how to do this better by designing processes of ethical reflection, identifying and analyzing moral problems, resolving moral value conflicts, and creating healthy, ethical peacebuilding organizations. Chapter 2 starts by acknowledging some significant barriers that exist in peacebuilding practice which inhibit ethical deliberation in our work. With these barriers in mind, a "doable" approach to ethics is proposed. "Doable" ethical reflection is tied to an action-reflection cycle to facilitate creating the mental and physical space for regular ethical check-ins in the midst of field work. Chapter 3 explores moral values in greater depth. In this chapter, elements that influence the content of our moral values, such as religion as well as our social, political, and conflict contexts, are examined in order to recognize the complexities involved in moral value discussions in divided communities. Chapter 4 explores moral theories and what they have to offer to practitioners in order to help think about various aspects of morality that may be relevant to our work. The moral theories that are explored are called duty-based ethics (or deontology), consequentialism, virtue ethics, ethics of care, and Ubuntu ethics. Chapter 5 delves into creative problem-solving techniques to consider using when moral values conflict. These creative problem-solving techniques draw upon conflict resolution methodologies as well as creative thinking methodologies. Chapter 6 recognizes that much of our peacebuilding work involves organizations and it is therefore important to also think about what makes for a healthy ethical organization and how we might structure practices in the workplace to support ethical peacebuilding practice. Chapter 7 steps back from examining the individual pieces involved in ethical thinking and action, and puts them together with summative guidance for easy reference in the midst of applied peacebuilding.

One final note, before we move on. A book about ethics runs the risk of being deemed unethical itself—this could be the case, for example, if it imposes a set of values with respect to what is good and right. This is an important critique because we are talking about, thinking on, and discerning values and their implications for peacebuilding work that occurs within many places and moral communities. As you read, keep thinking about your own moral values, the moral values of those around you, and how they fit the moral values and ways of understanding moral values in peacebuilding initiatives. Ask questions, question assumptions (including my own), and use points of disagreement and tension to explore the terrain more deeply in order to help your own decisions be more ethical.

FOR FURTHER EXPLORATION

The questions below are to help you think further about the issues raised in this chapter. These questions can be used for group discussion in the classroom or workplace, or they can simply be for you to ponder as you get started thinking more deliberately about ethics in peacebuilding:

- What are some of the values that drive you in your work for peace? Do you think of them as moral positions? Why or why not?
- When you reflect back on your work, when were the times when you have been a dogmatist, a relativist, or a rationalizer? If you have routinely been one of these, what were the effects of this on discussions about the issues at stake?
- What is problematic with offhand self-justifications or rationalizing? How does dogmatism affect conflict transformation? How might you

counteract these types of thinking in a discussion of ethics with colleagues?

- Whom do you know personally that you consider to be an excellent example of an ethical person? What makes this person stand out to you? What is it about his or her approach or actions that make him or her ethical? In what way is your example of an ethical person similar to examples that other people come up with?
- Have there been times when you've felt ethically compromised? What happened? Why do you think it happened? What would you do differently if you could?
- Choose one of the following scenarios and work on the skill of developing questions before answers. Read the vignettes and list the questions you might raise about what is being considered good and right in the peacebuilding initiative and the context that is described. Think about what you don't know and what would be helpful to know in order to more fully understand the problem being presented, and possible ways forward.

Scenario 1: Violence erupted in a city where an organization had supported peace work for ten years. The organization debated pulling out its staff and moving them to the head office in a city that was about four hours away. Community partners reported that the presence of the organization helped defuse violence and prevented false rumors from producing massive displacement in at least two neighborhoods. Community partners did not want the organization to leave. The organization was concerned for the safety of its staff members, and the risk assessment indicated that while it could reduce some risks to staff, it could not guarantee their safety. *What questions do you have about what is considered right and good? What other information do you need to further understand the context and the moral problem that is described?*

Scenario 2: A peacebuilder with established ties to government officials, military officers, and militant groups was asked to be an intermediary. In his first "official" meeting with the military leaders in the area the officers indicated their precondition for working with the intermediary was that he provide them with information about the militant groups. Indirectly they inferred they were looking for information on the militants' location, size, and armaments. Upon meeting the rebel leaders, the intermediary found he was pressed for the same information but this time with regard to the military's location and armaments. *What questions do you have about what is considered right* *and good? What other information do you need to further understand the context and the moral problem that is described?*

NOTES

1. This vignette comes from a discussion in 2012. Identifying details are removed for reasons of confidentiality.

2. The United Nations Security Council's 2001 Resolution on Afghanistan, S/Res/1386 is available in full on the United Nations website at: http://www.un.org/Docs/scres/2001/sc2001.htm. For a more detailed assessment of the relationship between aid, security, and the role of PRTs in Afghanistan, see Paul Fishstein and Andrew Wilder's report "Winning Hearts and Minds? Examining the Relationship between Aid and Security in Afghanistan" (Medford, MA: Feinstein International Center, 2012).

3. Sevérine Autesserre has done careful research which documents some of the worst effects of outsiders coming in designing peacebuilding projects or programs at a distance that misunderstand the conflict context and harmfully impose visions of peace to the determent of local peacebuilding and the local population. See, for example, "Hobbes and the Congo: Frames, Local Violence, and International Intervention" (*International Organization* 63:249–80; 2009) and *Peaceland: Conflict Resolution and the Everyday Politics of International Intervention* (New York: Cambridge University Press, 2014). For further examples of critiques of peacebuilding as it relates to colonialism or neocolonialism, see Roland Paris's article "International Peacebuilding and the 'Mission Civilisatrice'" (*Review of International Studies* 28 (4):637–56, 2002) or Susanna Campbell, David Chandler, and Meera Sabaratnam (eds.) *A Liberal Peace? The Problems and Practices of Peacebuilding* (New York: Zed Books, 2011). For an exploration of some of the limits of local peacebuilding, see Mary B. Anderson and Lara Olson's report "Confronting War: Critical Lessons for Peace Practitioners" (Cambridge, MA: CDA, 2003); this project notes that while grassroots peace work is valued, it is often critiqued for being of limited effect because it fails to change larger sociopolitical dynamics.

4. The definition of peacebuilding draws on Lederach, particularly *Building Peace: Sustainable Reconciliation in Divided Societies* (Washington: USIP Press, 1997). Johan Galtung's definition is provided in "Three Approaches to Peace: Peacekeeping, Peacemaking and Peacebuilding" (in *Peace, War and Defence—Essays in Peace Research*, vol. 2: 282–304; Copenhagen: Ejlers, 1976). The United Nations first definition of peacebuilding appears in Boutros Boutros-Ghali's report, "An Agenda for Peace: Preventive Diplomacy, Peacemaking and Peacekeeping" (New York: UN doc. A/47/277–S/24111, 1992).

5. The discussion of dogmatism, relativism and rationalizing in the chapter builds on Anthony Weston's *A Practical Companion to Ethics* (fourth edition, New York: Oxford University Press, 2011).

6. The exploration of moral values draws upon Weston's *A 21st Century Ethical Toolbox* (third edition, New York: Oxford University Press, 2012, p. 86).

2

"Doable" Ethics in the Field

In this chapter we explore doable ethics for peacebuilding practitioners. "Doable" refers to ethical deliberation that is tied directly to practice: something we engage in as part of our usual work, rather than an add-on that sounds nice but is unrealistic. To further our thinking about ethics during practice, it is useful to begin with practice. The following story helps ground this chapter in field realities and some of the ways in which ethical deliberation tends to unfold, which is poorly; it is a story that involves the unintentional negotiation of key moral values among workshop facilitators in the midst of a three-week peacebuilding training and planning workshop. After exploring three general challenges that arise in everyday work, a reflection-action cycle for ethical deliberation is proposed. The relationship between an ethics reflection-action cycle and evaluation is then discussed. The chapter closes with a return to practice through the example of an organization's ethical deliberations using a consensus-based model of decision-making in the midst of an assignment to monitor elections and accompany local activists.

FALLING BACKWARDS INTO ETHICS

In 2004 I worked as a peacebuilding technical advisor for a large American Catholic private voluntary organization engaged in international relief and development work. My job focused on fostering high quality peacebuilding programs, either as stand-alone or integrated programming within the organization's relief and development work.

One morning, I walked into headquarters following an overseas trip and was urgently packed off to join a workshop we were hosting in nearby Hagerstown, Maryland to try to help "get it on track," as I understood my task. The workshop was part of a three-week training and planning visit involving a delegation of twenty-one Burundians chosen by the Catholic Episcopal Conference of Burundi (CECAB) to form a peacebuilding commission. It was a unique collaborative effort between the United States and Burundian Catholic Bishop's Conferences and the organization I worked for, Catholic Relief Services (CRS). The aim for CRS was to support the Burundian Catholic church in its ability to develop a vision for, as well as the capacity to build, peace in their conflict-riven state.

The Catholic Church in Burundi is quite large, with some 62 percent of the population of nine million identifying as Catholic according to 2008 estimates. The Burundian Catholic church was active in peace initiatives, including dialogue with leaders of rebel and political groups, as well as developing a Center for Research, Education and Development to undertake social analysis and promote nonviolence, peace, and reconciliation. Catholic Relief Services had worked in Burundi for many years, and had supported the development of the Center for Research, Education and Development among other initiatives. CRS was eager to continue to support the Church in furthering its peace and justice work in the aftermath of violence in 1993 during which roughly 300,000 civilians were killed, half a million displaced, and a similar number of people became refugees in neighboring countries. This three-week workshop, only part of which took place in Hagerstown, involved a mix of spiritual reflection, training in trauma and conflict transformation, envisioning a peace and reconciliation action plan for the Burundian Catholic Church, as well as solidarity visits with various Catholic groups in the United States.

CRS required additional financial resources to support peacebuilding work in Burundi, due to its own budget limitations. The U.S. Agency for International Development (USAID) proved to be an interested partner, particularly given the size and geographic reach of the Catholic Church in Burundi. Peacebuilding work fit with USAID's interests in promoting peace and stability in the country and region. While CRS funded the initial three-week workshop, elements of the larger action plan were to be funded by USAID.

There were at least three sets of actors interested in how the workshop in Hagerstown progressed. These sets of people engaged the workshop differently, and held divergent values in terms of assessing and choosing what was right and good to do. These differences were heightened during the segment of the workshop that focused on future planning. Our divergences in values produced significant tensions, and my being packed off to Hagerstown was a manifestation of the tensions.

One set of actors—which included representatives from CRS and the Bishop conferences—organized, facilitated, and participated in the workshop. For them, a central dimension of the workshop focused on providing a nurturing space for participants to step back and process their deeply personal experiences with conflict and trauma, and to engage with their spirituality and faith community as part of a healing process. This was a necessary, foundational step before the group could move forward with a peacebuilding process within the Burundian Catholic church. A central component of the workshop for this group involved a moving and transformative spiritual encounter guided by a French Jesuit retreat master. This relationally and spiritually focused part of the initiative was developed by members of religious orders from the United States and Burundi, and it involved delving into spiritual practices as well as nurturing relationships of solidarity between the United States and Burundian Bishop Conferences. It was further undergirded by Catholic social teaching's principle of subsidiarity, with a commitment to ensuring that those closest to a problem, and who have a better understanding of an issue, were supported by those further away from the problem to effectively respond.

A second set of actors were those wanting to ensure the planning part of the workshop produced a project that was technically sound and would generate significant effects. This group largely consisted of CRS staff, particularly those who liaised with USAID on grant funding and knew its funding formats and requirements. My participation was requested by colleagues who wanted to be sure this initiative produced a technically proficient and appropriate proposal for a USAID-funded peacebuilding project that would be in addition to a solidarity relationship between the Bishop conferences. I was to help ensure that a substantive plan for peacebuilding was produced—one that could be implemented within a three-year time horizon. This meant that I and other colleagues, also drawn in belatedly, injected project planning, analysis and design exercises into the original facilitation format to ensure they generated a technically sound future implementation plan.

While we tried to respect the spiritual and relational process elements that the original facilitation team had established, our focus was on ensuring the end product was "proficient" and "realistic." This meant we were bringing in a set of values and associated activities that the original facilitation team had not prioritized and therefore produced conflict. We fell backwards into what was actually a conversation about values but without being able to name our values or talk clearly about them. We were frustrated, held competing mandates, and muddled through. The workshop planning sessions indeed produced a plan and a project. Yet, as Bill Headley and I observe elsewhere, "Both the desire for resources and the eagerness to give them . . . can badly distort the proper functioning of subsidiarity" (2010, p. 137).

The third set of actors with their own values operating were those working for the U.S. government who were concerned about the relationship this initiative had to USAID objectives. They were concerned with questions like: Did this initiative fit into an appropriate model of peacebuilding and statebuilding with which the U.S. government wanted to be involved? USAID is the development agency of the U.S. government and housed within the Department of State; it notes that foreign assistance has the twofold purpose of improving lives within developing countries and furthering American interests. USAID values the formal separation of church and state as a moral good; thus, funding a religious-based effort entered into murky and problematic terrain. The foreign policy aims of producing a stable, democratic state within the international community spoke to the moral good of the state itself (not the church) for preserving international order and development progress, and the need for technical expertise to ensure the effective delivery of these expected outcomes.

The workshop became an unintentional site of competing moral values. Was care for participants, their healing and solidarity to be valued as a moral good over producing a concrete peacebuilding plan? Were secular activities to be valued over church-based activities? Was faith and spirituality itself valued or merely serving as means to an end? Were outside Western values more important than Burundian values? Was subsidiarity, a value espoused by the Catholic Church and CRS, being overshadowed by the values held by those connected to the funding resources? These were and are foundational questions about value tensions and moral choices that, in retrospect, I see we navigated only at the edges.

A plan was produced by the group, ultimately, and a program implemented and funded by USAID between 2004 and 2007. The group made an effort to balance several moral values, and found that bringing in a technical focus had merit in terms of strengthening the content of what was developed. More than 300,000 youth participated in various peacebuilding initiatives, 1,900 teachers were trained in peace education materials, 10,000 people participated in trauma healing activities, and "listening centers" were established. However, we also may have undercut the energy of the Catholic Church's transformative force because "the faith dimensions of the initial proposal were deleted or overshadowed" during those years (Headley and Neufeldt, 2010, p. 139).[1]

In hindsight, even in an initiative involving a faith-based body that works to be moral and ethical, we were hampered by being unable to articulate or speak plainly to the divergent moral values operating below the surface. It produced significant tensions that worked against our good intentions—and all three sets of actors did have good intentions, from those within the delegation to those asking about its technical quality to those asking about U.S. government support.

This Burundi initiative, while unique in its particulars, is not so different from other peacebuilding initiatives. The practicalities of our work drove our decision-making. We were all busy with multiple demands upon us, and so not at our most creative nor open in terms of thinking about values and how to meet multiple values simultaneously (thinking creatively would have greatly improved our decision-making). Where we sat in our respective institutions and social locations affected the values at the forefront of our thinking and what we thought was right and good in the moment, in the midst of the workshop. And, finally, it was when our values clashed that we noticed acutely that we had different assumptions operating regarding good ends and the right things to do. Some of these same features appear to be representative of larger trends in our field, which undercut our ethicality.

OBSTACLES IN THE FIELD: I WOULD THINK ABOUT ETHICS BUT . . .

In our busy, messy, and mundane work worlds, there are moral concerns and challenges that matter to people in conflict and to peacebuilders. Are we supporting things we think are good and have good effects? Do we do what is expedient if it means compromising a key value like participation? Do we risk travelling in an insecure area to mediate a conflict? Whatever we call them, moral choices are made in the field. As with the Hagerstown workshop story, we often do not think very well nor deeply about our choices because as practitioners we are constrained or challenged by the circumstances in which we work and relate to the nature of working in and on deeply-rooted conflicts.

Three notable obstacles appear to arise regularly in peacebuilding practice: (1) the challenge of time constraints given busy practitioner schedules; (2) the concern that ethical reflections may lead practitioners down winding rabbit trails and off course from their work tasks; and (3) the issue of "staring into an abyss" and making already difficult issues more agonizing by talking about them and making judgments under duress. Each of these barriers requires careful consideration in order to develop a usable approach to ethics that enhances our peacebuilding efforts.

I have no time. One of the most significant constraints on peacebuilders in the field is time. There are a vast number of different types of initiatives in which practitioners might engage, ranging from community dialogue work, to physical and social reconstruction projects, disarmament and demobilization initiatives, to reconciliation and transitional justice efforts. Recognizing this diversity is helpful because it points to the varieties of actors we work with and the range of things we might do on a given day.

The scope and ambitions of peacebuilding, and findings regarding effectiveness, reinforce the time pressures that practitioners can feel. Evidence suggests that we seemingly need to address everything at once, or at least coordinate with others who work on other levels and components of social change to be effective and build long-term, sustainable peace.[2] To be effective at large-scale social change, we need to not only work with the grassroots but also connect with top-level leaders, we need to ensure that we not only focus on individual-level change but also target larger-scale sociopolitical change, and we need to work strategically to shift hinge points in complex systems. This demands constant networking and attention to multiple simultaneous processes.

The tasks one performs in peacebuilding also take place in highly charged areas, which further affects our perception of time. Even if a peace agreement is signed there are frequent "aftershocks" of violent conflict. This means that there are regular, unnerving incidents, such as armed confrontations between militia groups or youth, which can escalate into larger-scale conflict and to which peacebuilders must continually respond. Dealing with the unexpected requires immediate attention and occurs on top of demanding workloads. Our perception of time is affected as urgent matters take precedence and crowd out other things to which we also need to attend, such as finding funds, managing project timelines, writing activity reports, nurturing partnerships, and responding to the everyday problems and requests that require our attention.

In sum, peacebuilding practitioners have many demands upon their time, and work under difficult circumstances with high expectations for social change, which further compounds our feeling that we are pressed for time. Adding ethical reflection to these demands seems impossible.

Yet, even if we are not thinking about it, we are making value choices. In the Hagerstown facilitation conflict we were making recommendations for how to move forward based upon our respective moral values regarding what was good and right to do, whether that was personal and communal healing, technical proficiency or the separation of church and state. This meant that our values were imposed through decisions and actions without conscious awareness, and these values were in part problematic and contradictory to the aims we held in common as peacebuilders. In a sense we lost time because we were not able to articulate and address the problem head on.

Another short example of a moral failing occurring in part due to perceived time pressures is provided in textbox 2.1. This is a story about a young man's efforts to build bridges between internally displaced persons (IDPs) and local farmers, where the outcome did not match the held values. A young, well-intentioned man acted quickly to respond to a pressing problem in what turned out to be an inopportune moment. There is some additional nuance

TEXTBOX 2.1. JUST A BIT OF LAND TO GROW SOME FOOD

Matt* was a well-intentioned, resourceful, and likeable young volunteer working in Latin America in an area with an internally displaced persons (IDP) camp during the 1980s. The IDPs were displaced because the military suspected them of supporting the guerillas and had therefore burned down their village. The IDPs had little access to food, and so Matt decided to approach a local farmer with considerable landholdings to ask whether he might spare some land for the IDPs to use to grow food. He also hoped that this initial bridge-building activity might set the stage for more community relationship-building between the IDPs and villagers. Matt thought he was lucky when he ran into the farmer on a bus traveling back from the city to the village one day, and so he made his request then and there. Problems were pressing and action was required. The farmer, being placed in an awkward position, agreed. Matt was delighted and the IDPs began to till the soil.

What Matt missed was that the bus was not a private venue for conversation. Their conversation was overheard and interpreted as further evidence that the local farmer supported the IDPs and therefore the guerillas. As a consequence, the farmer was "disappeared." It was a devastating outcome. Matt, too, was labeled suspicious and taken by the military for questioning. The outcome was nowhere near the intended good. Matt had asked the farmer as soon as he saw him because it was expedient, and the IDP needs were pressing. It was a decision that Matt deeply regrets.

---

*Name is fictional.

to this story, however the textbox captures the core dilemma. In this case, a choice was made based on values with which many can easily identify (helping IDPs to grow food and perhaps develop relationships with a community). The action produced negative consequences that weren't contemplated in the time-saving moment.

In retrospect, we see our mistakes. Matt, as well as the actors involved in the Hagerstown facilitation example described earlier, all acted under time pressure. Acting under pressure compounded problems in complex conflict settings. When we act under time pressure we fail to fully consider our actions and often make poor choices that have negative consequences. In these cases, we are further behind than we would have been had we made time to articulate and weigh alternatives to produce wiser actions.

I don't want to run down rabbit trails. A second, related constraint on ethical thinking is fear that focusing on ethical considerations will lead people down winding trails without any clear direction or contribution to peacebuilding work. Rabbit trails provide an apt metaphor for this concern as they meander; rabbits also can leap from side to side to break up their scent trail, which means they are hard to follow; they will not lead you directly where you hope to go, and you can spend a lot of time searching them out. There are two intertwined issues here. One is a concern that the amount of time spent considering ethical issues will detract from the amount of time available to engage in activities producing the desired outcomes, which is related to the time point discussed above. The second concern is that the focus of discussions will not necessarily be related to desired actions and outcomes. The discussions themselves might lead people astray.

A concern that ethical considerations will lead people off track is an important matter as it speaks to a tension between thinking and action, and the need to provide parameters to ensure that ethical analysis and dialogue is focused on application—this is even a problem that students in my class on the ethics of peacebuilding encounter in simulations designed specifically to consider ethics in peacebuilding (see textbox 2.2). Academics, too, are susceptible. As a practitioner returning to academia, I have found that the deeper I get into a particular moral theory, the further I'm drawing from practice as I try to make the best—the tightest, most logical, and most well-reasoned—argument rather than respond to the complexities of the situation before me. Rigorous application of one or more moral theories is time consuming and not always helpful when people are trying to engage in ethical peacebuilding daily.

This means we need to be discerning about the way we engage in our ethical thinking, putting in place some guides that keep us thinking creatively and connect us to how we do our practice directly. It speaks to the need for balance between ethical action and ethical reflection. In the Hagerstown story or in Matt's story we can see that some well-timed, focused explorations of important moral values, deeper understanding of the contexts and moral value tensions, as well as the development of alternative options for our actions that could satisfy multiple moral values would have significantly improved the good achieved in and through our work.

I cannot stare into an emotional abyss. Because peacebuilding occurs during and in the aftermath of violent conflict, we work with men, women, girls, and boys who have witnessed, experienced, and participated in violent acts such as mutilation, rape, or ethnic cleansing. Most of us, given our druthers, would prefer not to hear about these acts let alone be confronted

TEXTBOX 2.2. TOO MUCH ETHICS?

In simulations with time pressures and quasi-real challenges, people get to experiment with different formats of ethical reflection that might fit within a work environment. In some peacebuilding simulations I have run, participants have designed ethical reflection systems that require them to rigorously analyze every decision they make using four or five different moral theories (more on this in chapter 4). They very deliberately consider different moral theories and compare them and the decisions they would respectively yield. When groups do this they find they are not able to make timely decisions, and sometimes belatedly realize that they weighed issues for a very long period of time that were actually not very relevant to their decisions.

This experience in the protected environment of a simulation setting reinforces an important insight for doable ethics in the field: we need to craft processes for weighing moral concerns that encourage open questioning and at the same time move us deliberately towards application. We need someone or some process to keep us focused on our task and still ask big questions.

repeatedly and regularly with stories of them. Working with victims and perpetrators of violent acts exposes practitioners to some of the worst in humanity. Hearing these stories can be psychologically and emotionally deadening. Many peacebuilders also have lived through violence and war and carry their own stories and trauma. Work environments can further contribute to emotionally stressful conditions, with damaged physical infrastructure making office space and travel challenging.

It is important to recognize that it is profoundly difficult to work in the aftermath of a war because it leads to an additional set of important considerations about when and how to think about ethics. Given the pain and suffering already witnessed by practitioners, we can understand questions like: Do we really want to think about the ethical dimensions of our own actions further? Aren't we already doing good by engaging in peace work? Do we have to think about what we might be doing wrong? What if there is no "right" answer but only the lesser of two wrongs? Do we really need to stare deeper into this abyss of problems?

These are tough issues to think about. Sometimes the most ethical thing is to say "I can't talk about this issue right now" because we are not able to analyze aspects of our work at that point in time. Peacebuilders who suffer from trauma—whether primary or secondary—may find that when we talk about what we value, what happened or might happen, then we can draw close to an emotional abyss. Self-care is sometimes overlooked in the field of peacebuilding as the stakes for many people are so high, and yet self-care is very important. Ensuring we care for ourselves as well as those with whom we work is an important feature of ethical peacebuilding.

Knowing yourself, your team, and the context in which you work will all shape when and how you engage in ethical deliberation. Your first moral decision may in fact be about how to ensure that ethical reflection is good for, and not detrimental to, people. This might mean adding additional listening opportunities in order to hear where people are at, or allowing some people the space to withdraw and choose not to participate in discussions at a particular moment in time, even if others need to deliberate. Textbox 2.3 provides an example of a small team's ethical deliberations in which people were given an option to not participate in discussions, and where some team members dealing with trauma after witnessing mob violence found they were heard and understood in new ways by colleagues through the conversation. It may be helpful to note that in thinking about moral values, even in grim circumstances, we are making a positive choice and choosing to support things that we do think are right and good. Just as when we listen to those who have experienced and lived through violence and war, we also hear stories of compassion, generosity, and love. They are not mutually exclusive.

"DOABLE" ETHICAL REFLECTION

Establishing a process of reflection that is "doable," and helps us as well as others, is important if we are going to enhance the ethicality of our peacebuilding. It needs to be timely, it needs to be focused without foreclosing questions, and it needs to respect where people are at emotionally. This requires thinking about ways that we can create space—mental and physical—within the rhythms of our workdays and workweeks to ask questions, to deliberate and decide what is most ethical, to act, and to assess. A light and flexible cycle of action and reflection therefore appears most suited for the task.

Action-reflection models are a mainstay of reflective practice in conflict transformation as well as learning organizations. They are useful to help individuals and teams be adaptive and responsive within the context of complex social change initiatives.[3] In these models, action and reflection continually feed each other. The regularity of reflection can vary and is something that is experimented with in order to find a cycle of reflection that works well for individuals, teams, and the conflict context. Reflection cycles can be daily, weekly, or monthly, and can vary in terms of depth of reflection. For example, a quick ten-minute personal daily reflection can be paired with an hour-long monthly team discussion of pressing issues. Action-reflection cycles are effective when they are regular processes and routines which contribute to healthy learning environments and healthy ethical climates for organizations, teams and communities—a topic further explored in chapter 6.

The reflection-action model presented in figure 2.1 highlights three main phases in the reflection process that can be used to draw-out ethical considerations: (1) inquiry and deliberation, (2) decision-making, and (3) assessment. Reflection is listed before action in this model because of the emphasis on moral values being at the core of action, and to which we need to attend as a foundation for ethical deliberation. Reflection is captured in the first two phases of the diagram. However, as evident in the example provided in text-box 2.3, reflection and action are often not separated as neatly as appears in the diagram, to which the "watch and adjust" label alludes. Yet to make sure that we are giving sufficient time and space to ask ethical questions in the midst of action it is helpful to separate them conceptually.

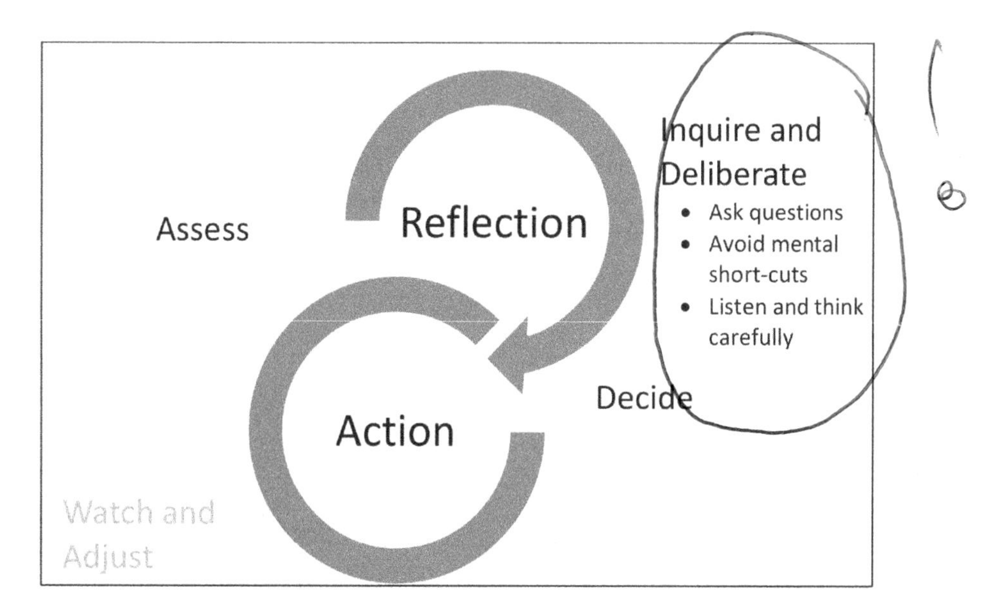

Figure 2.1. An Ethics Reflection-Action Cycle

We can enter iteratively into reflections on ethics at any point in action: before, during, or after. For example, many practitioners find themselves in the midst of action when they begin to feel a nagging sense of doubt or get an uneasy feeling in the pit of their stomach about what they are doing, which is what occurred in the Hagerstown example. If we had moved into a more conscious assessment of the situation and then articulated our values in order to inform our subsequent actions (which we did not quite manage), we would have entered into this cycle based upon our assessment of what went wrong, and then moved into inquiry and deliberation.

Inquire and deliberate. Open and careful thinking involves inquiring into and deliberating upon what matters, why, and for whom in the process of peacebuilding. It requires spending time asking questions, surfacing, and exploring moral values as well as examining how values are enacted or not enacted within our work. The "inquire and deliberate" phase builds upon the three foundational ethical thinking tasks identified in chapter 1: ask questions, avoid mental shortcuts, and listen and think carefully.

An important element within this part of our ethical reflection process is inquiring into our moral values at the core of our own and others' actions. Here we identify or name our moral values and ask deep and probing questions about the values we hold. We question where these values come from and explore what other values might be important to consider for ethical peacebuilding. We can ask questions about why particular values are understood to be important, and how it is that some values were institutionalized and others not. Or, whether or not some important values are marginalized or undervalued due to particular social power dynamics that inform how we prioritize values.

A related process is the deliberation over moral values—discerning what will guide our decisions within the context of the peacebuilding initiative in which we are working. Guiding values are the ones we use in order to make judgments regarding what is good or bad, right or wrong, just or unjust in our work in a particular context. Examples of guiding values are those listed in professional ethics guides, or those that are the focus of moral theories or religious ethics. Listening carefully to the context and people with whom we are working is also necessarily part of this process.

The process of identifying, exploring, and questioning moral values is often challenging, and is the focus of chapter 3. To assist us in the process of thinking systematically and openly about moral values, chapter 4 explores moral theories that can offer key moral values—or ways of thinking about moral values—for people and organizations to consider. Together the contents of the next two chapters function to deepen our ability as practitioners to inquire and deliberate on ethics in the midst of, before, or after action.

Decide. After identifying guiding values, it is important to choose actions that are informed by the moral values of all those involved. This step seems obvious, yet it is sometimes overlooked because we think that once we have articulated our values we are done with thinking ethically. Of course, acting ethically means that we act based upon a conscious decision about what is right, good, and just as we and other stakeholders see it.

Our decision-making context will affect our decisions. If we are in the midst of an escalating conflict, we need to be prepared to make a rapid decision, where at other times we might be able to take more time to decide an issue. Power and bureaucracy will also play into our decision-making process in different ways and affect which values dominate our decision-making process and therefore also need to be weighed. For example, the power of funds in the Hagerstown example altered the priority for more secular peacebuilding activities over spiritually centered practice, as well as the enactment of the principle of subsidiarity.

There may be times when we confront a difficult choice, and where we feel we must choose between two competing goods that appear unattainable at the same time. This is referred to as a moral dilemma. In peacebuilding, people are frequently faced with difficult dilemmas such as whether or not to put oneself at physical risk for what might be a greater good, or encourage others to take risks. Dilemmas are points of tension because we believe we can only achieve one value at a cost to the other. Yet, reality is complex and messy, which allows us to rethink most dilemmas and move from an either-or situation to one where creative alternatives can be generated;[4] creative-problem solving helps us to do this (for more, see chapter 5).

Wallace Warfield, a former conflict resolution practitioner and professor, advised people to consider three questions to help come to good decisions. First, how strongly you hold your personal values (e.g., how much does a value like participation as a collective good matter to you)? Second, how sharply does the situation you are confronting diverge from the values held in common by the profession of conflict resolution practitioners (e.g., are you being asked to do something that goes against a core value of your professional community)? And, finally, what have others done in situations similar to the one you are facing; are there moral exemplars you might draw upon? These are important questions for us to consider in order to help maintain our personal and professional integrity while also being responsive to the context.[5]

Establishing in advance a procedure to follow in order to make decisions about moral values is a final feature to consider as it can smooth the ethical decision-making process. To return to the Hagerstown example, *if* we had established a loose stakeholder reflection group to weigh in on value considerations then we would have better responded to our dilemma; in this alternative scenario, representatives from the workshop, as well as the facilitators and USAID funders would have a direct voice in an important conversation about values and might have envisioned something entirely new for how to proceed, which we as a smaller facilitation group were unable to imagine. Once a deliberate decision is made, then it is time for action.

Act, watch, and adjust. At times, we name our moral values or principles and engage in action, but then encounter problems living them out in our work. For example, we aspire in a peacebuilding project to having the community make decisions about peace and reconciliation processes in their community, and yet insist on home-office approval in North America (or Europe or elsewhere) for modifications to the budget. Or, we aspire to the principle of full community consultation in setting up a project, but find we are trying to develop a proposal for a donor by the donor's deadline and so run out of time and just put our own ideas and those of a few key community leaders into the project. These are examples of when our deeply held values are overtaken by other values such as efficiency or accountability. In these cases, we may not recognize what has happened, or we might have simply cut short our ethical thinking with a quick, self-serving rationalization.

Action is *not* an all-or-nothing proposition. It is always possible to make adjustments mid-way through an initiative. In the midst of our work, we can stop, engage in a quick (or long) reflection on our moral values and ask: are we really living out our values here? Is there another way to do things that might be better? We can use our values to steer our moral and ethical behavior while in motion just like we use the handlebars of a bicycle to steer while we ride. These mid-course corrections are what keep us on the road.

Assess. After our action, or during a scheduled break in action, we can assess how we are doing with living out our moral values. It is here when we are more likely to ask whether we are acting upon the *right* values. We can also ask whether or not our actions really did contribute to a greater good, and whether we did things right in the process. Assessment here is in part about looking at ends—which we can see after we are finished—as well as assessing our means, the characteristics that we embody along the way, and the ways in which we related to each other in the process. This language sounds similar to evaluation, and our reflection-action ethics cycle may be directly connected to evaluation if an organization has well-developed learning and evaluation processes that include discussions of values, which is explored in the section below. Whether part of formal evaluation or a check-in on moral values performance after one part of an initiative is complete, assessment feeds into another cycle of reflection and action as we learn in order to improve the ethicality of our future action.

To conclude, the reflection-action cycle proposed here is a conceptual tool to help each of us think about when and how to step back and create the space for questions, thinking, and informed decisions. The type of reflection-action cycle each of us finds "doable" depends in part upon us and our personal preferences, as well as our context and organizational structure. Incorporating and improving those practices we already have in place, such as existing action-reflection activities, or monitoring evaluation and learning systems, will help ensure ethical reflection is indeed doable.

CONNECTING ETHICS AND EVALUATION

Monitoring and evaluation in many organizations is intended to be a rich part of internal learning, although the practice does not always evince this. Monitoring and evaluation cycles, or reflective practice cycles in developmental contexts, can include purposeful ethical reflection and provide a natural home for "doable" ethical reflection. The following section examines some of the connections that can be made between evaluation and ethical deliberation.

Evaluators collect empirical data, analyze, and interpret it in order to make judgments about a program or project's worth, merit, or value. Deborah Fournier notes in her definition of evaluation for the *Encyclopedia of Evaluation* that "it is the value feature that distinguishes evaluation from other types of inquiry, such as basic science research . . ." (2005, pp. 140–41). Values are the heart of ethical deliberation, and it may not be surprising that value judgments are often the most contentious part of evaluations, particularly when different stakeholders hold values that they feel were not respected or considered in the judgments made by an evaluator. Within evaluations, we ask questions like: What were the intended and unintended effects of what we did? Did we do the right things to build peace? Were our effects good? These are weighted and political questions for many because they involve values regarding what constitute good, and these value judgments are typically connected to accessing resources following the evaluation.

If we are using evaluation as part of purposeful ethical deliberation, then there are three sites in the evaluation process at which conversations about ethics can be meaningfully enhanced. The first conversation focuses on who determines the values and criteria by which we judge programs. This conversation requires consulting multiple stakeholder groups, including the larger moral community in which the intervention occurs.[6] It may be primary stakeholders who initiate this conversation, or the evaluator who ensures a discussion of values occurs with stakeholders. If it is the evaluator, his or her role is not to pre-judge the values, but rather to help stakeholders identify what is most important, worthy, and meritorious through dialogue and can be part of the process of developing a focused Terms of Reference.

The second, related, conversation is about the big questions of what constitutes "good peacebuilding" or peacebuilding "done right." This is a conversation that initially happens when a peacebuilding initiative is envisioned and it is returned to and rearticulated in evaluation, Terms of Reference, or Scope of Work documents. Deliberation about the moral values guiding judgments of worth and merit is frequently left to those who design the Terms of Reference, which is then used to hire an evaluator. Designing the Terms of Reference or Scope of Work for an evaluation can therefore be an important point where thoughtful ethical deliberation can be meaningfully expanded.

A third conversation is with respect to the evaluation methodology itself, and ensuring its process is ethical. This involves being sensitive to the conflict environment during the evaluation as well as taking care to ensure the methodologies and ways in which people are engaged are ethical—for example, considering ways in which the inquiry process is systematic, the evaluator is competent and demonstrates integrity, and the evaluation process is respectful of people. A number of resources developed specifically to assist people in thinking about ethics in evaluating peacebuilding initiatives are listed in the Notes section.[7]

In some peacebuilding interventions, evaluation itself is part of an ongoing reflective process that occurs with developmental evaluation. In these processes the evaluative learning cycle provides a strong and natural platform for ongoing "doable" ethical deliberation. In other situations, evaluations occur infrequently. Therefore, while most evaluations can provide an opportunity to thoughtfully explore ethical questions connecting ethical deliberation to evaluation processes, having evaluations in place presents only a partial response to our challenge of "doable ethics."

I *CAN* THINK ABOUT ETHICS!

Each of us already engages with ethical questions at some level, even if it is when we fall backwards into a discussion of ethics or judge the merit of our program during an evaluation. Others of us think about ethics only when we have dramatically failed, or once we've stepped back from intensive engagement, perhaps months or years later. In textbox 2.3, there is an example of a team's deliberation process which was structured to engage ethical questions during the midst of action. It provides an idea of how a team considered moral issues carefully in a reflection-action cycle. While the deliberative process was not perfect it offers a model of practical ethical thinking in situ.[8]

TEXTBOX 2.3. REFLECTION-ACTION WITHIN A PEACE BRIGADES INTERNATIONAL TEAM

Peace Brigades International (PBI) is a civil society organization that provides nonviolent accompaniment for local activists whose lives are threatened. The organization began in 1981 and is similar to other nonviolent accompaniment organizations that engage international staff and volunteers as observers in order to protect and stand with local activists. Other examples of organizations engaging in similar work are Christian Peacemaker Teams, Nonviolent Peaceforce, and the International Solidarity Movement. PBI, the oldest of this group, is guided by the principles of non-interference in terms of the organizations they accompany, and non-partisanship in terms of engaging with multiple parties with an open mind. It also foregrounds consensus decision-making that reflect its Quaker roots.

The following paragraphs explore how PBI engaged in ethical deliberation as part of a team consensus decision-making process in Sri Lanka in 1994. The descriptive material of the decision-making process comes from Patrick Coy's work, which uses an ethnographic approach to document and analyze PBI's accompaniment model. I have folded an ethics reflection-action analysis into Coy's rich description. While Coy does not frame his analysis in terms of ethics, he offers a detailed account of a decision-making process in which careful ethical deliberation occurs and therefore a working model of "doable" ethical deliberation.

In 1994, long-term and short-term PBI team members were in Colombo discussing guidelines for monitoring elections. The short-term team members had arrived to help monitor Parliamentary Election Day violence. Sri Lanka was in the midst of a hotly contested and difficult election process marked by "disappearances" and intimidation. As part of the PBI orientation and logistical planning session, longer-term team members presented the new arrivals with a set of guidelines for their engagement. The guidance included the statement: "if the situation turns violent and uncontrollable, leave the area" (Coy, 2003, 105). Given the focus and mandate of the organization, and their principled commitment to accompaniment and nonviolence in the face of violence, some of the new arrivals strongly disagreed with this guidance. A conflict over moral values ensued. Those who had drafted the guidelines were also principled in their reasoning and drew upon experiences in

(continued)

Sri Lanka with a chaotic violent incident in which they felt their international presence had made absolutely no difference; they therefore valued protecting life (others and theirs), and effectively protecting local actors over the long-term. The guidance was the product of their initial moral assessment based upon reflection after a troubling incident during the candidate nomination process.

The disagreement over the guidance to "leave the area" was important for the PBI team to process as it involved significant matters of moral principle and their very reason for being in Sri Lanka. In response, the team held two additional meetings to discuss their values in the context of personal risks, fear, and direct experiences of violence. These two meetings occurred as soon as they could be scheduled following the emergence of the conflict. The original tension emerged in the midst of a morning logistics meeting, after which the team went on to other tasks.

The first follow-up meeting was therefore scheduled as an optional meeting at 10 p.m. that same day. Almost all of the fifteen members attended. The small group facilitating the meeting began with an exploration of team members' thoughts and beliefs regarding the nature of nonviolence, which meant that the conversation necessarily foregrounded ethics and their conceptions of what was morally good and right for them as international PBI observers in Sri Lanka at that time. Their discussion of moral values preceded discussion of application in terms of the problematic guideline, and enabled a thoughtful and respectful conversation in which the team explored the meaning of their work and why it was important. They drew upon personal experiences as well as other values, such as trust and relationships, to process the principles and actions at stake in the problematic guideline. For example, Coy quotes one young long-term member saying:

> I don't have anything against the spiritual approach, but I am essentially a political person. I may be different from some of the rest of you. I don't know. But I do know I am here for the long haul. No, actually I am not just here for the long haul, I am in the struggle for justice for the long haul, and that struggle just happened to place me here in Sri Lanka for this period of time. I am here for expressly political reasons, and I am no martyr. One can't be a martyr and be in these struggles for the long haul. (2003, p.108)

Others responded to this comment by sharing their own experiences of taking risks, and thanking the young man for sharing his feelings. An older, short-term member directly responded, "I have always thought of myself as a long haul person," and this did not mean ". . . you cut corners in your work, or that you don't take serious risks. It means that you take a longer view of the goals and objectives of your work" (quoted in Coy, 2003, p. 109). These types of comments, and sharing of personal experiences, were threaded through the conversation as people expressed themselves, affirmed each other, and provided alternative views of what moral action required.

After meeting for about an hour and a half, they came to a general consensus (described below), and decided to hold a follow-up meeting the next morning to further process their feelings and fears before heading-out to their respective monitoring assignments. The morning meeting was structured as a sharing circle, in which each member had one opportunity to share their greatest fear(s) and hope(s). This circle sharing brought their disagreement to a close with a final opportunity for deep personal sharing and connection, which facilitated understanding, joint ownership of their task as well as strengthened team cohesion.

In the end, the team came to a working consensus on action based upon their common moral values without redrafting the guideline. The group roughly agreed that if the violence was coming from police, they would stay as they believed they could have an effect on that violence, but if the violence was coming from unruly factions then they would leave as they were unlikely to be effective. They also included the caveat that it was each team member's decision whether to stay or leave.

This sense of the group reflected three strongly held moral values: first, they engaged in accompaniment work in order to be effective and limit violence, and that achieving their ends successfully was an important feature of "good" work; second, challenging violence with nonviolence was important and "right" on its own terms for some team members, regardless of effectiveness; and third, each individual was valued and expected to make his or her own decisions regarding risk.

The open and careful discussion process which occurred through the three meetings enabled moral values to be articulated and affirmed, to expand the range of behavioral options to PBI members operating with similar moral values, and to generate agreement while respecting differences of moral values. Following the meetings, the team disbursed to their respective tasks and locations.

The PBI example in textbox 2.3 is instructive for our purposes of thinking about a responsive reflective-action ethics cycle. The team enacts moral reflection and ethical deliberation within their regular work schedule. The initial guidance for action came after reflection; it was then further reflected upon by the team, which expanded their understanding of ethicality for the team and enhanced their options. In this case, the team responded to a moment of crisis, which generated add-on meetings even in the face of time pressures. The meetings were held quickly at times that were less than ideal but they enabled the team to maintain its intensive work schedule and partnership commitments. The meetings themselves were carefully structured in order to surface moral values, value emotions and personal experience, and respond respectfully to members of the team. This allowed the members of the team who had experienced pre-election violence to express themselves and be heard by newer members of the team. In this way, they carefully negotiated the emotional abyss. The facilitators also enacted procedures in their consensus-based process to ensure that team members were not pressured to come to a premature or false position of full agreement by allowing for context-based decisions, and personal choice. In this way, they enabled open questioning while still moving the group towards agreement. Finally, the organization had a decision-making model in place that everyone on the team respected, which meant that they did not waste time debating decision-making procedures but moved immediately into discussions of key moral values.

Finding a reflection-action process that works and integrates into our regular work routines is the task of doable ethics. The PBI example is just one model, and is incomplete. Things to consider, in addition to those drawn out by the example, are how to engage in ongoing ethical reflection in the midst of routine work and how to engage stakeholders outside of an intimate team in ethical decisions (e.g., bringing-in Sri Lankan partners into PBI's deliberations). Experiment and explore ways in which ethical deliberation might be more meaningfully engaged in your own work based on the nature of the intervention, the team or organization as well as the context. In the following two chapters we further explore moral values and how to engage in open and purposeful conversations about moral values to provide further ideas for *what* to think about during ethical deliberation.

FOR FURTHER EXPLORATION

Here are some questions and activities that you can use to further think about issues raised in this chapter:

- Develop a list of your core peacebuilding values. What is important for guiding your choices about what is good and bad, right and wrong, just and unjust in the field?
- The chapter discusses three barriers to ethical reflection that appear to be common for peacebuilders. In what ways are these barriers relevant to you? What other barriers do you think exist that might negatively affect thinking about ethics in the field? Are there ways to overcome the barriers?
- What are some ways or strategies that you've used to date to think about moral values in the field? How have these worked? Were there negative or positive effects?
- The team ethics decision-making example provided in textbox 2.3 employs the use of consensus procedures to develop agreement amongst members of a team for what is right and good to do. In this case, the team proceeded with a general common understanding and allowed for differences of understanding amongst team members—leaving decisions up to each individual. What are some strengths of this model of decision-making for discussing moral values? What are some limits or weaknesses of this model?
- Design an ethical reflection process for yourself and a team of four peacebuilders. How regularly will you reflect on the ethics of your work? What kinds of questions will you ask? How will you make decisions when values conflict?
- Alternatively, design an ethical reflection process for the Hagerstown workshop group. Who should be involved in an ethical reflection-action group? How could the reflection-action be structured to surface and deal with moral value differences?

NOTES

1. A longer description of the work with the Burundi contingent as well as description of the Burundi conflict is contained in William Headley and Reina Neufeldt's "Catholic Relief Services: Catholic Peacebuilding in Practice," in *Peacebuilding: Catholic Theology, Ethics and Praxis,* edited by Robert J. Schreiter, R. Scott Appleby, and Gerard F. Powers (Maryknoll, NY: Orbis Books, 2010). Burundi's religious identification and population figures come from 2008 data, which was reported in the CIA World Fact Book and available at: https://www.cia.gov/library/publications/the-world-factbook/geos/by.html. USAID's purpose and connection to U.S. foreign policy is described on their website at: http://www.usaid.gov/who-we-are. I should also note that the Burundian church continued to engage in its own peacebuilding work after the events described here, and my analysis is circumscribed.

2. The findings regarding effective peace practice and the need to work at the sociopolitical level with more and key people come from the Reflecting on Peace Practice Project, written up by Mary Anderson and Lara Olson Anderson in *Confronting War: Critical Lessons for Peace Practitioners* (Cambridge, MA: CDA Associates, 2003).

3. For general discussions of action-reflection cycles and the power of reflective practice, see Donald Schön's classic book *The Reflective Practitioner: How Professionals Think in Action* (New York: Basic Books, Inc., 1983). For a nascent exploration of the connection between self-reflection, practice, and ethics, see Marc Gopin's section on "self-reflection at the core" in *Bridges Across an Impossible Divide* (New York: Oxford University Press, 2012, p. 626).

4. Anthony Weston is a philosopher who draws upon conflict resolution literature to help reframe dilemmas and opposing arguments into expansive problem-solving, which is helpful in turn for peacebuilders; see particularly his book *Creative Problem-Solving in Ethics* (New York: Oxford University Press, 2007). For a different perspective than the one offered here regarding ethical dilemmas in the field, see Hugo Slim's chapter "Dealing with Moral Dilemmas" (in *Peacebuilding: A Field Guide*, edited by Luc Reychler and Thania Paffenholz; Boulder, CO: Lynne Rienner Publishers, Inc., 2001).

5. These three questions and an alternative ethical reflection model are presented in Wallace Warfield's "Is It the Right Thing to Do? A Practical Framework for Ethical Decisions" in *A Handbook of International Peacebuilding: Into the Eye of the Storm*, edited by J. Jenner and J. P. Lederach (San Francisco: Jossey-Bass, 2002). Cynthia Cohen has produced a workbook called *Working with Integrity* for peacebuiders engaged in coexistence work that is particularly helpful when considering the ethics of listening (Waltham, MA: The Brandeis Initiative in Intercommunal Coexistence, a program of the International Center for Ethics, Justice and Public Life, Brandeis University, 2001).

6. For thinking about different communities of accountability and how to bridge them, see Larissa Fast, Reina Neufeldt, and Lisa Schirch's article "Toward Ethically Grounded Conflict Interventions: Reevaluating Challenges in the 21st Century" (*International Negotiation*, 7 (2):185–207, 2002). Deborah Fornier's comment appears in the definition of evaluation in the *Encyclopedia of Evaluation*, edited by Sandra Mathison (Thousand Oaks, CA: Sage Publications, Inc., 2005). Michael Quinn Patton provides a cogent discussion of "power, politics and ethics" in chapter 14 of *Utilization-Focused Evaluation* (fourth edition, Thousand Oaks, CA: Sage Publications, Inc., 2008).

7. For example, see the articles by Kenneth Bush, Colleen Duggan, and Janaka Jayawickrama in the special issue on evaluation in violently divided societies in the *Journal of Peacebuilding and Development* (8 (2): 5–41, 2013).

8. General information on Peace Brigades International, their mission, operating structure, and principles is available on their website at: http://www.peacebrigades.org/. The example in textbox 2.3 is drawn from Patrick Coy's writing, particularly his articles "Negotiating Identity and Danger under the Gun: Consensus Decision Making on Peace Brigades International Teams" (*Consensus Decision Making, Northern*

Ireland and Indigenous Movements 24:85–122, 2003) and "Shared Risks and Research Dilemmas on a Peace Brigades International Team in Sri Lanka" (*Journal of Contemporary Ethnography* 30:575–606, 2001). Any errors in interpreting the ethics of the decision-making process in Colombo are my own and not Coy's. Finally, if you are interested in reading more on different models of nonviolent accompaniment, a broad overview is provided in Howard Clarke's edited volume *People Power: Unarmed Resistance and Global Solidarity* (London: Pluto Press, 2009).

3

Values, Values Everywhere

Moral values identify things that we consider important, or of worth, which we use to determine (judge) what is right or wrong, good or bad (morality). Anthony Weston defines moral values as those values that speak to our and other's legitimate needs and expectations (2013, p. 86)—he uses the criteria of legitimate needs and expectations as setting the standard by which we judge what will be right and good. This definition leads to the question: Who defines legitimate needs and expectations? This is a great question and answering it is an important part of what philosophers as well as communities and societies deliberate upon.

As moral communities we decide together the content of our moral claims, and in so doing establish what constitutes legitimate needs and expectations. For example, life—being able to live—is understood to be a legitimate need (and expectation) of ourselves and others. This means, on the whole, we believe we should all be allowed to live without the threat of being killed by others. This is understood to be right and good for all of us. It is only under exceptional circumstances, such as war, when this moral value is abrogated, and even then we have sought to circumscribe exceptions to this moral good through mechanisms like the Geneva Conventions to provide protections for civilians as well as prisoners of war. Other examples of moral values that philosophers draw upon are fairness, respect, equity, justice, and care. Note that these move us beyond base expectations of legitimate needs, such as food or shelter, and into questions of what it means for us to live well and flourish together.

In this chapter, we delve further into understanding moral values in order to better identify moral values, understand ways in which our moral values are shaped by the communities in which we live, as well as how conflict contexts may affect our moral values. Identifying moral values is not difficult but it does require building or honing our listening skills so we are able to hear and name values. The chapter begins by exploring moral values that are embedded within the technical language used to describe peacebuilding. What complicates our discussions of the ethicality of peacebuilding work is that moral values are affected by where and when we live, and we often are working across or between communities. The chapter therefore explores the relationships between moral communities and moral values. This includes a discussion of religious sources of values, as well as an exploration of the ways in which power and social context shape moral values. Conflict contexts provide an additional layer of complexity to understanding moral values, and an internal conflict in East Timor in 2006 provides a focal point for a case study of the dynamic interaction between conflict and the way in which the moral value of resistance has been shaped over time. The chapter concludes with an exploration of ways by which we can identify values in multifaceted, delicate social settings in order to act ethically, whether in our own moral community or in another's moral community.

WATCHING FOR "GOOD" (AND "BAD"): RECOGNIZING AND NAMING VALUES

Frequently peacebuilders ask: "How can we stop further violence and move toward peace?" In response, we hear answers like: "let's work to establish positive relationships across conflict lines to start building social trust"; "let's promote a traditional community mediation process to ensure conflicts are managed locally within communities"; or "we need to demobilize and reintegrate former guerilla fighters and military members back into the community to decrease the likelihood of post-war violence." These types of responses present thoughtful ideas about what people might do to contribute toward building peace. We usually listen to responses like these operationally because they tell us what we can concretely do in order to change things. For example, they tell us we need to work with divided groups, traditional mediators, or former fighters. If we work on peacebuilding projects regularly, we might also hear how much time or funding the project will need to support the initiative being proposed (e.g. twenty years, five years, two years). These are operational concerns we are l,istening for that effect how, when, and with whom we engage. This lens, however, presents only one way of seeing the picture.

For many years, I thought I was thinking operationally, proposing particular projects based upon a technical assessment of the situation. This was how

I approached the Burundi workshop that was described at the start of chapter 2. This was important as it was my job to ensure that our initiatives were building upon what we knew about effective peace work in order to avoid repeating errors and engaging in bad practice. Yet viewing interventions only in that way meant I was overlooking all the value judgments my colleagues and I were making regarding what was worthy, desirable, and right to pursue—and conversely, what was unworthy, undesirable, and to be avoided. I paid attention to some values in terms of what constituted good technical peacebuilding practice and ignored others, such as nurturing the spiritual side of the Burundian group discussed in the preceding chapter.

Our value judgments speak to why we do the work we do, and what motivates us to choose particular courses of action. In the first answer above, "let's work to establish positive relationships across conflict lines to start building social trust," we see that positive social interchange is considered desirable, worthy, and right to pursue; and, further, constructive or positive social relationships between the groups in conflict are right and good ends. In the second statement, "let's promote a traditional community mediation process to ensure conflicts are managed locally within communities," we see local leadership and local participation in managing conflicts as right and good, and therefore worthy to pursue. In the third statement, "we need to demobilize and reintegrate former guerilla fighters and military members back into the community to decrease the likelihood of post-war violence," it is the prevention of future outbreaks of violence that is considered desirable, right, and good. Judgments of right and good are embedded in our operational language, as well as in our evaluation language (as discussed in chapter 2).

In order to listen for value judgments that are implicit in the ideas we generate, and choices we make in our peacebuilding work, we can not only look at what is proposed as a good end but also at how we are framing problems in our conflict or context analysis—that is, how we determine what is wrong and needs to be changed. We can listen carefully to what people *say* is good and right, as well as what people *assume* is widely understood as good and right in these analyses. Conversely, we can also listen for what people say is "bad" and "wrong." While listening, we need to be open to disparate points of view to ensure we are not being blinded by our own assumptions of good and right.

The following example will help get us started. Textbox 3.1 contains a statement in full issued by the Burundi Configuration (subgroup) of the United Nations (UN) Peacebuilding Commission in spring 2015.[1] It is an aspirational statement as well as one intended to send operational signals to Burundian leaders regarding upcoming elections, and it provides an assessment of what is problematic in Burundi as of its writing. It was written during

TEXTBOX 3.1. THE SITUATION IN BURUNDI: STATEMENT BY THE BURUNDI CONFIGURATION OF THE UN PEACEBUILDING COMMISSION

15 May 2015
(Reprinted here in full)

New York, 15 May 2015—The PBC Burundi Configuration[1] met today to hear an update on the situation in Burundi by the Permanent Representative of Burundi, H. E. Mr. Albert Shingiro, as well as by the UN's Under-Secretary-General for Political Affairs, Mr. Jeffrey Feltman. Today's meeting of the PBC Burundi Configuration has been its third since 29 April 2015.

The PBC Burundi Configuration highlights the importance of dialogue and reconciliation among all Burundians to address the root causes of the current crisis. It stresses the need to find a lasting political solution that ensures Burundi's hard gained progress in peace consolidation and peacebuilding.

The PBC Burundi Configuration calls on all Burundians to urgently establish, through open dialogue and a spirit of compromise, the necessary conditions for the holding of free, transparent, credible, inclusive and peaceful elections.

The PBC Burundi Configuration welcomes, encourages and fully supports continued regional engagement in Burundi, particularly by the East African Community, the African Union and the International Conference of the Great Lakes Region, with a view to finding a lasting solution to the crisis.

The PBC Burundi Configuration equally commends UN efforts, particularly through the Special Envoy of the Secretary General for the Great Lakes Region, Mr. Saïd Djinnit, and MENUB [United Nations Electoral Observation Mission in Burundi]. It fully backs the Special Envoy's mandate.

The PBC Burundi Configuration will continue to follow the situation closely and stands ready to help Burundi at this critical juncture of its journey towards sustainable peace and development.

NOTE

1. The Configuration is composed of the following countries, UN representatives and regional and international financial institutions: Australia, Bangladesh, Belgium, Bosnia Herzegovina, Brazil, Burundi, Canada, Chad, Chile, China, Colombia, Comoros, Croatia, Democratic Republic of the Congo, Egypt, Ethiopia, France, Germany, Guatemala, India, Italy, Japan, Kenya, Malaysia, Mexico, Morocco, Nepal, Netherlands, Nigeria, Norway, Pakistan, Republic of Korea, Russian Federation, Rwanda, South Africa, Sweden, Switzerland, Trinidad and Tobago, Turkey, Uganda, United Kingdom, United Republic of Tanzania, United States, African Union, East African Economic Community, Economic Commission for Africa, Economic Community of Central African States, European Union, Executive Representative of the Secretary-General, Food and Agricultural Organization, International Conference on the Great Lakes Region, International Monetary Fund, Inter-Parliamentary Union, Organisation internationale de la francophonie, Organization of Islamic Cooperation, Special Representative of the Secretary-General for the Great Lakes Region, World Bank.

a time when the president of Burundi had decided to stand for elections a third time, shortly after a failed coup attempt, and during a time of heightened tensions and escalating violence. The president's decision to run for a third time was highly controversial and argued to be against the 2005 constitution. Read the statement and identify moral values that you see.

This statement houses a number of important claims about what is understood to be commonly agreed upon as good and right given the legitimate needs and expectations of Burundians as well as others in the Great Lakes Region and the international community. The community of supporters for the claims of what is good and right in this document are understood to be those listed as members of the Burundi Configuration group in the note, which notably includes national United Nations representatives such as ambassadors from Australia, Bangladesh, or Switzerland (the chair), as well as United Nations officials, representatives of regional institutions of various types (e.g., Organisation Internationale de la Francophonie, African Development Bank, African Union, European Union) and international financial institutions that are part of the United Nations system (World Bank, International Monetary Fund). This Configuration, therefore, represents a set of international actors speaking into Burundi—an interesting element of moral values engagement in peacebuilding to which we return shortly.

The articulation of moral values begins most obviously in the second paragraph. Nonviolent means of dispute settlement are valued as right and good in the phrase, "dialogue and reconciliation among all Burundians to address the root causes of the current crisis." The emphasis on nonviolent dispute settlement is returned to in the third paragraph, with its call for "open dialogue and a spirit of compromise." A political solution is understood to be the right technical response, which relates to the value of political order and stability held by the Burundi Configuration and the United Nations more broadly. A necessary condition for political order is more carefully specified in paragraph three and entails "the holding of free, transparent, credible, inclusive and peaceful elections." In this sentence several values are espoused, including nonviolence, participatory democracy, and transparency. These are understood to be good and right means and respond to the legitimate needs and expectations of Burundians as well as the PBC Burundi Configuration representatives. There is a statement about good ends in the document, which is embedded in the final phrase: "sustainable peace and development." There is also a strong statement about the wrong thing to do, which is to undermine or lose the "hard gained progress in peace consolidation and peacebuilding." Finally, there is an assertion that it is right and good for this set of international actors to speak into Burundian politics and to expect that Burundi will respond to this set of concerns. In sum, nonviolent dispute settlement, political order and stability, participatory democracy, transparency, sustainable peace and development are some of the main moral values presented in the reading above—you might identify others in addition to this list.

Identifying why actors choose to act—our reasoning or justifications for why we think it is important to act—helps to understand the moral values that are guiding actors' decisions, as does identifying the way in which a problem is framed. Further, by understanding the context from and in which these values emerged we see how our values are related to social, political, and even economic factors. The way I introduced the context of Burundi, just prior to textbox 3.1, emphasized problematic political dynamics. The same occurs in the letter itself. This framing of the problem emphasized political order as a moral good. This is an important claim and is understandable given the actors and context in which they are speaking; it is, however, a limited moral claim. It did not speak to other important components of what it means for Burundians to flourish, including personal well-being and recovering from trauma, relational healing, and nurturing community—all of which were important for the Burundi contingent referred to in the preceding chapter.

The moral values espoused by the Burundi Configuration are rooted in its UN institutional context. The claims made regarding what is right and good for Burundi reflect the Charter of the United Nations itself, and the expectations and moral standards that were enshrined therein in 1945—and therefore expected of all member states. The values of peace, avoiding war, promoting international stability and a particular type of social progress are clearly laid out in the preamble of the Charter, and reinforced in its various articles. For example, Chapter VI, Article 33 emphasizes the value of nonviolent dispute settlement (1945) as a central means to ensure the "moral end" of stable order: "The parties to any dispute, the continuance of which is likely to endanger the maintenance of international peace and security, shall, first of all, seek a solution by negotiation, enquiry, mediation, conciliation, arbitration, judicial settlement, resort to regional agencies or arrangements, or other peaceful means of their own choice." The value of order and stability between states is further emphasized and enshrined in the UN Charter with Chapter VII's provisions for the Security Council to determine what measures to take in response to any threat to peace, breach of peace or act of aggression, from the use of sanctions to the use of full military force.

The UN Charter was drafted during World War II by allied powers who anticipated winning the war, and was in part based upon the values of the allied western states and lessons from the failures of its predecessor organization the League of Nations. The allied "great powers"—Britain, France, the Soviet Union, and the United States—initially envisioned themselves as overseeing security decisions and actions to ensure a stable, global political order; these four, plus China, privileged themselves in the nascent organization by establishing five permanent seats in the body responsible for overseeing international security, the Security Council. The values upon which the United Nations was based drew from largely European and American sources (indeed, the preamble to the UN charter begins with the phrase "We the people," mirroring the U.S. Constitution). That said, there were also strong norms of non-intervention and non-interference in sovereign states, which were also embedded in the UN Charter. The Burundi declaration, therefore, comes only after significant shifts occurred in the international system after the demise of the Cold War, and in a context of increasing acceptance of international intervention post-1992.[2]

Peacebuilding efforts regularly respond to particular problems such as post-war trauma, severed relationships, or a weak and poorly functioning state. Depending upon how we frame a problem, we move particular value-based claims to the fore. Is the problem a lack of order? A lack of justice? Listen to how problems are framed, as well as what is left out, to help identify moral values and listen to not only the strongest voices but also those that might be quiet or disadvantaged. In listening, we should not be surprised to find actors articulate different, important values which speak to broad and context-specific concerns based upon their vantage point and context (e.g., a tendency by international actors that value international stability, and grassroots actors to value the quality of life in their location).

Further, how we understand our moral values and their application may change over time. The example of moral values and changes in how slavery was understood is illustrated in textbox 3.3. At times we will need to suspend our own judgments and listen to disparate points of view, explore an issue from different angles, and find out more information. By asking questions and engaging openly and carefully we avoid the mental shortcuts of relativism, dogmatism, and rationalization, as well as enact the moral value of respecting people. Once the values at stake in a given decision are identified, we can engage in fulsome ethical deliberation.

UNDERSTANDING MORAL VALUES IN CONTEXT: MORAL COMMUNITIES

Throughout this book, I use the term "moral communities" in the plural. Some philosophers, such as Richard Rorty, use the term moral community to refer to a bounded group of people that trust one another and believe they are of equal moral worth.[3] If you are in a moral community then you are considered worthy of response by others in that community, and if you are outside of it you are not entitled to the same opportunities, assistance, or rights. The approach that Rorty and others take is helpful in terms of identifying the politics involved in moral choices around setting the boundaries of "who we are," which is particularly important when we think about distributing resources or responding to the needs of others. For example, do we respond only to those in one's neighborhood? Economic class? Religious community? Ethnic group? Nationality? State citizenship? Or species? This discussion invokes considerations of power and choice, which are centrally important for ethical action—choosing who is considered in or out of one's moral community is a powerful act that needs to be interrogated. Tim Murithi notes in *The Ethics of Peacebuilding*, reconsidering one's enemies as morally worthy and bringing them into one's moral community is itself an important aspect of peacebuilding and reconciliation. These are important considerations around moral community, yet I have chosen to use a slightly different definition for this book as part of a bridge-building strategy as we think about *how* to think morally.

I use the term moral community to refer loosely to groups of people who hold similar moral values together. This approach to understanding moral community foregrounds a need to listen to, understand, and engage with what is valued locally in order to recognize a moral community. It also suggests that in order to operate in and between multiple moral communities we need to listen to and engage with more than one set of moral values and not presume a single moral community. It does not follow from this premise that those within the moral community only believe these values apply to themselves, although that may be the case. I take this approach because in peacebuilding we work to build peace within and between moral communities. For example, in the Burundi Configuration, several overlapping layers of moral community could be identified: the United Nations–centered community (which sees itself as universal), Burundi as a collective whole, as well as the contested subgroups within Burundi with distinctive moral claims. Rather than assume there is commonality of claims, this approach emphasizes the possibility of difference, and therefore the need to be attentive to those around oneself within a contested setting and their respective values.

Moral communities may be small or large as they are defined by moral value commitments rather than numbers or geographic borders. From this perspective, moral communities may overlap like circles in a Venn diagram; people who live in different moral communities, with distinct social histories and cultural practices, may hold similar moral values. Their similarity opens space for the possibility that we may have moral values that hold across time and place, or what some call universal moral goods. The discussion of the moral value of reciprocity in textbox 3.2 highlights an example of one such moral value that resonates with many religious traditions around the globe.[4]

However, moral communities may also understand or enact their moral values very differently. For example, even while the value of reciprocity is held in common by many traditions, there are differences in the framing of this value, with one set of quotes framing reciprocity as a positive action (do the same to others) and another set framing reciprocity as involving not doing something, or a negative action (do not do to others). This framing of a positive or negative demand affects how people think and act upon this moral value, as does understanding the religious tradition from which the respective quotes come, as well as the expectations and practices of the community. We need to identify and think carefully about moral values and how they are practiced within and between moral communities for ethical peacebuilding.

Many of us are not fully aware of all that shapes our personal moral compasses as our values are (often subliminally) absorbed from the moral communities and social worlds in which we live. Our religious, cultural, socioeconomic, and historical contexts are important pieces of the puzzle in understanding *how* we think about good and right as well as *what* we think is good and right. The relationships between moral values, religion, power, and conflict contexts need to be examined in order to help us think about questions of whose values we are considering, and how these values relate to considerations of social justice in peacebuilding decision-making.

TEXTBOX 3.2. A RESONANT MORAL VALUE: RECIPROCITY

There are significant debates around on whether or not there are universal moral values. Even if one takes a position that there are no universal moral values, one can easily identify some values that resonate across many contexts. One of these values is reciprocity. Jeffrey Wattles explores this value in his book *The Golden Rule* (1996), which has been popularized on websites and posters. Below are a set of religious texts from Wattles' work that echo the value of reciprocity:

- "One should never do that to another which one regards as injurious to one's own self." *Mahabharata* 13, 113 (p. 191).
- "Tzu-kung asked, 'Is there single word which can serve as the guiding principle for conduct throughout one's life?' Confucius said, 'It is the word "consideration" [*shu*]. Do not impose on others what you do not desire others to impose upon you.'" *Analects* 15.23 (p. 16).
- "It happened that one came to R. Akiba and said to him, 'Rabbi, teach me the whole Law all at once.' He answered, 'My son, Moses, our teacher, tarried on the mountain forty days and forty nights before he learned it, and you say, Teach me the whole Law all at once! Nevertheless, my son, this is the fundamental principle of the Law: That which you hate respecting yourself, do not to your neighbor. If you desire that no one injure you in respect to what is yours, then do not injure him. If you desire that no one should carry off what is yours, then do not carry off what is your neighbor's.'" *Shabbath* 31a (p. 60).
- "None of you [truly] believes until he wishes for his brother what he wishes for himself." *An-Nawawi's Forty Hadith* 13 (p. 4).
- "All things therefore which you want/wish/will that people do to you, do thus to them for this is the law and the prophets." *Matthew* 7:12 (Wattles translation p. 54).

RELIGION AND MORAL VALUES

For many, it is religious sacred texts, leaders, and communities that are the sources of their moral values as well as the locations within which ethics are discerned, debated, and enacted. Even if a peacebuilder's orientation is more secular, he or she will find that peacebuilding work often engages with and within religiously defined moral communities. How do we think about the relationship between religion and moral values as peacebuilders who work with religious moral communities, which may be divided?

Within religious traditions the source of moral values is God, Allah, or a greater divine universal power. For example, Christian ethics reflect on moral issues based upon Christian beliefs about God, the Bible, and to varying degrees theological exegesis, as well as traditions and experiences. For Muslim ethics, the Quran provides the direct word of God, and is complemented by the Hadith, which provides a record of the Prophet Muhammad's life and traditions. Jewish ethics are rooted in the sacred word of God in the Torah and the Tanakh; this wisdom is complemented by the oral tradition captured in the Talmud as well as rabbinical Midrash writings.[5] These are rich sources of religious moral teaching for Christianity, Islam, and Judaism, and there are many other sacred sources that are likewise important for other religious and spiritual communities, such as the Mahabharata, the writings of Confucius or Guru Granth Sahib.

While sacred sources and traditions provide strong moral guides, the moral statements or commands require interpretation. The moral value of reciprocity, noted above in textbox 3.2, provides an illustration of a moral value that requires interpretation. What does reciprocity actually mean when one is making a decision, such as how should I respond to those displaced by conflict in Syria as an outsider living in Canada (or any other country)? Or, how should I respond as an insider to the problem of being implicated in a system of cultural genocide in Canada, as recently articulated by Canada's Truth and Reconciliation Commission's final report on Indian Residential Schools? What should I start doing to enact reciprocity? What should I stop doing? Determining the answer to these questions takes consideration and interpretation. If I am a member of a religious community (in my case, Mennonite), religious teachings and the faith community help me to discern what is right.

Religious leaders, such as priests, rabbis, or *ulama,* are sources of wisdom and interpret holy texts. However, how they do so varies across traditions. Even within one group, such as Catholicism, there is tremendous variation in practices of interpretation—in that case ranging from Papal authority that may be invoked, to layers of interpretation offered by priests, to theological writings, as well as lay Catholic communities which may further interpret scriptures and teachings among themselves. The process and practice of interpretation is shaped by the religious community, its tradition, and context, and there is often significant internal debate over how to interpret and apply moral commands. What this means for us, when working across or within religious traditions, is that the meaning of religious teachings are not self-evident and requires careful thought and exploration—ethical deliberation—as well as knowledge of the religious group with whom we are working.

It is clear that when working in and on conflict with members of religious communities, and discussing moral values, the choice of what terms to use matters. What terms will enable peacebuilders to speak together about moral values and be understood? At times I have found it important to use first-order religious language to capture the religious dimensions of moral claims within the community. However, at other times I have used secular terms in order to avoid contested meanings associated with the first order religious language, and to avoid implying things I did not intend as an outsider. As you think about what language to use and how to engage with religious moral communities on ethics questions in peacebuilding, some questions to consider are: What terms are most appropriate for those with whom I am working? Will the terms clarify? Will the terms suggest I have a particular position within the discussion? The next chapter explores four moral theory perspectives, which use what might be called second order language for religious communities, in order to examine a set of important moral value claims. These moral theories are informed by, or resonate with, religious traditions but are shaped more clearly by philosophical traditions that have distanced themselves from religious ethics.

POWER AND VALUES

Power is understood here broadly as influence which alters people's decisions and actions. Sources of power might be expertise, financial resources, position, or the ability to reward and punish. While most peacebuilding initiatives try to be participatory, there often is a dynamic of inequality implied by where the funding is coming from (e.g., outside versus inside funders), or those leading the peacebuilding initiatives (e.g., coming from more powerful social classes with more educated backgrounds). This sets up a dynamic where power is imbalanced, and those who design and lead peacebuilding initiatives are better resourced than those in the community who are supposed to live out the peace; those with expert and financial power are in an inordinately strong position to set goals and decide where benefits will accrue vis-à-vis poorer members or those on the receiving end of an initiative and the decisions. Part of our ethical deliberation, therefore, involves being attentive to power, the ways it is manifest, the ways in which our work interacts with different groups and affects resource distribution.[6]

There often are powerful institutions and systems in place shaping what we think is right and good. For example, the Burundi Configuration letter illustrates the power of the United Nations family of institutions in shaping what is considered right for international actors. Not everyone's values are equally represented and respected by powerful systems and institutions—the 2007 UN Declaration on the Rights of Indigenous Peoples is an example of a document that seeks to modify some of the value claims represented by the UN via respecting collective values for indigenous groups.[7] The political nature of moral value decisions (in deciding who or what is worthy of receiving goods and what types of goods) suggests we need to understand where our values come from and what is at stake within different value systems for ourselves and for those with whom we work.

The relationship between institutional power and moral values is often difficult to see because it involves questioning things we might take for granted as normal at the time, or questioning sources we think are authoritative. It also requires that we look at what we assume to be good more generally in our cultural context. For example, slavery during the nineteenth century was argued to be a moral good. This example, explored in greater detail in textbox 3.3, is helpful because it is something that many clearly understand to be morally wrong today. Yet, John C. Calhoun, who served as a U.S. vice president, secretary of state, and as a senator from South Carolina in the early to mid-1800s, thought it was morally right. He provides a clear example of someone living at a certain time and place, whose appeals to authoritative moral commandments were significantly informed by the social and economic context in which he lived. Calhoun was not alone, and he was viewed as an articulate leader for the South at the time.[8]

There were strong economic, political, and social interests at stake in maintaining the institution of slavery. Slaves made labor-intensive crops like tobacco and cotton profitable. The international slave trade was abolished in 1808, and northern states in the United States abolished slavery before that date, however the final Emancipation Proclamation that freed all slaves in the United States was issued in 1863, during the American Civil War.

When we interpret and seek to apply our moral values, there is an important place for questioning and discernment with respect to the effects of power and privilege. It was the questioning of values that abolitionists were engaged in, which helped people to see slavery as wrong. We also know that questioning deeply held values, which may alter economic or political power between groups, can contribute to escalating a conflict. Those in the abolitionist movement were viewed as troublemakers. This included former slaves like Frederick Douglass and Sojourner Truth who were eloquent spokespersons for emancipation. It also included voices from the South like Angelina Grimké who, as a member of a slaveholding family, had benefited from the system and yet whose moral compass was shaped differently than Calhoun's. In contrast to Calhoun, she (along with her sister) argued that "The laws of Moses *protected servants* in their rights as *men and women*, guarded them

TEXTBOX 3.3. VALUES AND POWER: DEFENDING SLAVERY AS A MORAL GOOD

In 1837 John C. Calhoun, then senator from South Carolina, argued that slavery was a positive good. Calhoun's views on slavery were supported by many within institutional churches based upon interpretations of the Bible and an ordained and benevolent hierarchy. Here are some quotes from Calhoun's famous February 6 speech on the floor of the United States Senate in which he morally justifies slavery on behalf of the South (full text available online, see Notes section). Calhoun's speech comes in response to petitions from abolitionists. Read these passages and identify the ways in which the social and economic context shape Calhoun's moral justification for slavery:

> To maintain the existing relations between the two races, inhabiting that section of the Union [the South], is indispensable to the peace and happiness of both. It cannot be subverted without drenching the country in blood, and extirpating one or the other of the races. Be it good or bad, [slavery] has grown up with our society and institutions, and is so interwoven with them that to destroy it would be to destroy us as a people. But let me not be understood as admitting, even by implication, that the existing relations between the two races in the slaveholding States is an evil:—far otherwise; I hold it to be a good, as it has thus far proved itself to be to both, and will continue to prove so if not disturbed by the fell spirit of abolition. I appeal to facts. Never before has the black race of Central Africa, from the dawn of history to the present day, attained a condition so civilized and so improved, not only physically, but morally and intellectually.
>
> . . . I hold that in the present state of civilization, where two races of different origin, and distinguished by color, and other physical differences, as well as intellectual, are brought together, the relation now existing in the slaveholding States between the two, is, instead of an evil, a good—a positive good. . . . I hold then, that there never has yet existed a wealthy and civilized society in which one portion of the community did not, in point of fact, live on the labor of the other. Broad and general as is this assertion, it is fully borne out by history.
>
> . . . There is and always has been in an advanced stage of wealth and civilization, a conflict between labor and capital. The condition of society in the South exempts us from the disorders and dangers resulting from this conflict; and which explains why it is that the political condition of the slaveholding States has been so much more stable and quiet than that of the North.

from oppression and defended them from wrong. The Code Noir of the South *robs the slave of all his rights* as a *man*, reduces him to a chattel personal, and defends the *master* in the exercise of the most unnatural and unwarrantable power over his slave . . ." (2000, p. 271). As part of this "troublemaker" abolitionist movement, Grimké was warned she would be arrested if she ever returned to South Carolina after distributing an abolitionist letter to "Christian women of the South" in 1836. This same threat was ever-present for former slaves.[9]

The example of slavery helps to highlight that what we—and others within our community—understand to be right and good is affected by power and our context, and that our understanding of what is good can and does change in important ways over time. We can also be people "of our time" and engage in careful ethical discernment as Grimké's actions demonstrate.

It is difficult to question our own assumptions about what is good and right, particularly if we benefit from how these moral values are understood and enacted. Calhoun's argument for slavery supported an economic system that was ordered to benefit slaveholders. Grimké's questioning of slavery came from the perspective of someone who benefited from the economic system, but who was also politically disenfranchised as a woman without voting rights. Frederick Douglass and Sojourner Truth argued against slavery from their lived experience as chattel slaves, on the margins of society. In textbox 3.4, there is a quote from Miguel De La Torre, which asserts that our moral values are shaped more by our sociopolitical context rather than our religious or ideological beliefs. He argues that it is only from the margins where genuine critiques of unjust systems and structures emerge. De La Torre's comments can challenge us in peacebuilding to think about the values that we hold which may align with dominant powers that benefit from values in the midst of our peace work.

In peacebuilding interventions, and the policies that frame such interventions, we frequently see manifest some of the assumptions that De La Torre names as aligned with the dominant culture: the call for law and order, hyper-individuality, and an uncritical acceptance of the market economy in peacebuilding, which are often aligned with statebuilding policies. De La Torre challenges us to think about the ways in which these values may "reinforce prevailing social structures responsible for causes of disenfranchisement" (2013, p. 1). Our dominant assumptions may also include a preponderance for deductive ethical reasoning, such as that rooted in ends-based consequentialist or rule-based duty thinking (both are explored further in the next chapter). As peacebuilders, we need to carefully think through how the moral values we deploy are intimately tied to power, culture, and history if we are to be ethical practitioners.

TEXTBOX 3.4. QUESTIONING VALUES FROM THE MARGINS

From Miguel De La Torre's Introduction to *Ethics: A Liberative Approach*, p. 1 (Minneapolis: Fortress Press; 2013):

> I believe based on who I am. In other words, what I (as well as you) hold to be true, right, and ethical has more to do with our social context (our community or social networks) and identity (race, ethnicity, gender, orientation, or physical abilities) than any ideology or doctrine we may claim to hold. Those from dominant cultures usually find that the ethical worldview they advocate, forged within their social context before they were even born, is usually in harmony with maintaining and expanding the power and privileges they hold. In other words, even if an ethic is constructed within the dominant culture that is capable of critiquing and demanding reform of the social structures that privilege their race, ethnicity, gender, orientation, class, and/or ableism, it will seldom call for a dismantling of those very same social structures. As cutting edge as such ethics might appear to be, it would seldom threaten their privileged place in society.
>
> While the ethical positions held within the dominant culture are neither uniform nor monolithic, certain common denominators nevertheless exist, such as a propensity toward hyperindividualism, a call for law and order, an emphasis on charity, an uncritical acceptance of the market economy, an emphasis on orthodoxy, and a preponderance for deductive ethical reasoning. While such an ethics is congruent with the dominant culture, it is damning for those residing on the margins of society because of how it reinforces the prevailing social structures responsible for causes of disenfranchisement.

In Calhoun's speech, power over others, domination, and political order were defended as good. We also see this value of "power over" present in conflicts today—a direct contradiction to our frequently held conflict transformation value of "power with" people. In many places, young men and women gain social status and respect once they have power over other people. During violent conflict this becomes particularly acute, as those with the guns seem to have the power to decide what happens in a community—who will live or be killed, who will be raped or let be, who will eat, and so forth. We also see this in our international system, and sometimes people resort to violence because they feel those with official "power over" are treating them unjustly. The value of "power over" frequently persists even when the guns are off the streets: in bar fights, in the marketplace where those who have financial power set the rules, and in homes where men and women abuse those who are weaker than themselves. This presents a profound challenge for peacebuilders.

It is impossible to eliminate power dynamics in our work. However, we can put power and an assessment of power vis-à-vis values on the table as part of our ethical deliberation. We can even put the valuing of "power over"—the moral valuing of domination or benevolent hierarchy—on the table for us to explore given the challenges it presents in peacebuilding work. To put power on the table means considering how resources affect our work and shape the values we embrace. We can ask questions like: Whose values are we embracing? Why are these values important as compared to other values? Are there differences in moral values between those who benefit from this moral claim and those who do not? How are values implemented in policies? What do we do if we value equal participation but we think that what a marginalized group wants is misguided or even wrong? How do we enact a decision-making process to act more ethically?

VALUES AND THE LONG SHADOW OF CONFLICT: THE CASE OF EAST TIMOR IN 2006

What follows is a case exploration of one moral value in East Timor in order to better understand how and in what ways the long shadow of conflict shapes and is shaped by moral values. The example explores how East Timor's long history of opposing colonial occupation has shaped the moral value of resistance, and how valuing resistance as a good in turn shaped an internal conflict in 2006.[10] The example also touches on ways in which peacebuilding operational decisions interacted with the historical conflict context of East Timor and conveyed problematic ethical messages.

East Timor has a very long history of resistance, and resistance itself became the mark of a virtuous Timorese citizen during its quest for independence. Indonesia occupied East Timor for twenty-four years, and it is estimated that over this time period one quarter of East Timor's population, or 180,000 people, were killed or died as a result. This period, a part of lived history for many Timorese in 2006, was a critical formative experience and shaped the way the nation was framed. However, prior to Indonesian occupation, East Timor had been colonized by the Portuguese for almost 450 years, with a very brief period of independence in 1975. There was intermarrying between Portuguese and East Timorese which produced a *mestiços* elite. Yet, during this same time period, there was very little investment by Portugal in East Timor, and there was a long legacy of resistance against the European colonial power. As Armindo Maia, a former minister for Education stated in an interview:

> We have a common history of resistance; first against the Portuguese. There's a long list in the history of rebellions against the Portuguese. Then we have the history of resistance against the Indonesians. This unifies us. And I hope it will cement our determination to fight for a better future, to fight for a better life and society. There is broad support for this simple version, or notion of *fumu*. (quoted in Leach, 2007, p. 195)

Recognition of and homage to martyrs is captured in the constitution of East Timor. The preamble of the 2002 constitution enumerates three fronts of resistance in laudatory language: first the armed resistance front led by "the glorious Forças Armadas de Libertação Nacional de Timor-Leste (FALINTIL) whose historical undertaking is to be praised," second the clandestine front that "involved the sacrifice of thousands of lives of women and men, especially the youth, who fought with abnegation for freedom and independence," and thirdly the diplomatic front that paved the way "for definitive liberation." The preamble then states, "Ultimately, the present Constitution represents a heart-felt tribute to all martyrs of the Motherland." Embracing resistance as part of the moral fabric of the nation was furthered in section 11 of the constitution, titled the "Valorization of Resistance." In this section it states: "The Democratic Republic of East Timor acknowledges and values the historical resistance of the Maubere People against foreign domination and the contribution of all those who fought for national independence," and ensures special protection for those who dedicated their lives to the struggle for independence as well as recognizes the role of the Catholic church in the independence movement.

In 2006, there was significant internal conflict and a breakdown of political and security institutions in East Timor. There was massive displacement in the capital Dili, with roughly 70 percent of its population displaced at night and immediate calls for international assistance to re-establish order and to support peacebuilding. East Timor was a young nation at the time, and had begun its path to statehood after a referendum in 1999 when the majority of people voted for independence from Indonesia. Between 1999 and 2002 the United Nations temporarily administered East Timor, and then it became a fledgling, independent state in 2002.

In 2006, at the outset of the conflict, significant sociopolitical tensions between political leaders had simmered in a context of weak institutions, high poverty and unemployment, and its very long history of occupation and valorization of resistance. Many of East Timor's political leaders were known as heroes and warriors for independence. They were part of the resistance, whether political, military or clandestine activists, and had moved into elected leadership positions in the new state. In May 2006 this included President Xanana Gusmão, Prime Minister Mari Alkatiri, Foreign Minister José Ramos Horta, Brigadier General Tuar Matan Ruak, and Interior Minister Rogerio Lobato, to name a few of the key actors in the crisis.

In April 2006, then Prime Minister Mari Alkatiri fired nearly six hundred military personnel who had gone on strike protesting conditions for western East Timorese in the military. With this act, Alkatiri fired just under half of the total military force. The conflict spiralled, and the police force and military were divided and mired in accusations, with each seen as representing either the west or the east within East Timor and losing credibility with the other part of the population. In the crisis over thirty people were killed, and there was widespread displacement and unrest in Dili.

The conflict mobilized and polarized a longstanding internal division between those from the east and the west within East Timor. While there are roughly thirteen distinct ethno-linguistic groups, they are also clustered into larger social identity groups based upon geography; between those who live in the east or west of the country, referred to as *firaku* or *lorosae* (from where the sun rises), and those who come from the west, known as *kaladi* or *loromonu* (where the sun sets). This distinction was magnified and became more antagonistic in 2006 as part of escalating tensions. Each group was aligned with a position in the conflict—those aligned with the protesting military who were sacked were *loromonu*, and those aligned against them were *lorosae*. Dili was separated into *loromonu* and *lorosae* neighborhoods, markets, and internally displaced camps, where members of each group felt safe respectively. Some politicians attempted to remain in the middle, such as Xanana Gusmão and Ramos Horta, who in part could be in the middle because of their roles in the independence movement; however, it was a difficult place to occupy. In this division each side looked to defend their community, to be safe, to be recognized, and equally valued as resistance fighters for East Timor.

Part of the connotations deployed in the terms *loromonu* (or *Kiladi*), and *lorosae* (*Firakus*) relate to claims about the strength and potency of resistance (the terms also contain other connotations about character, such as being taciturn or emotional). Those who identified as being from the west suggested that those from the east did not resist Portuguese occupation as strongly as they did in the west, and easterners were coopted by the Portuguese. Those who identified as being from the east argued that those from the west did not resist Indonesian occupation as strongly as they did in the east, and that westerners were coopted by the Indonesians. In fighting to defend themselves, each argued they had resisted occupation more strongly than the other, and their respective sacrifices were greater.

Already in December 1999 and January 2000, in the early days of forming an independent nation, Dionisio Babo Soares documented clashes between youth that centered on the east-west division, respect and perception of their contributions to the resistance. Soares writes: "The young people of Bobonaro could not tolerate the insult from Laga that loromonu people did not participate in the fight against Indonesia during the twenty-four-year struggle. The fight involved swords and machetes. Interestingly, some former members of FALINTIL were also involved; joining with the firaku youths, but the International Forces stopped the fighting" (2003, p. 280). Soares further notes that this division was misinterpreted by United Nations personnel as gang violence, rather than recognizing the deeper divisions manifest. The frameworks of the United Nations statebuilding mission did not enable a full reading of the significance of this division and the content of the moral claim being contested, nor did it enable a full reading of the moral community and its values.

From 2000 forward, statebuilding and peacebuilding in East Timor was layered over two periods of occupation. Both periods of occupation had left significant physical and psychological scars and had shaped people's understanding of themselves, their society, and what was valued. The valuing of resistance as a virtue was a product of the history of anti-colonial resistance. This value played an important role in contributing to the escalation of the conflict in 2006, as each group sought to defend themselves against threats and insults from the other side. Many argue it was mobilized by political elites, which reinforces the significance of the claim of resistance and the degree to which it is tied to perceptions of excellence of character. The valuing of resistance as good and right was shaped by the long history of conflict, it was enshrined in the constitution, and it in turn shaped reactions to the crisis events in 2006.

As we think about moral values in peacebuilding, this example suggests that part of social change involves moral communities rethinking their own moral values and how they are enacted in the present. East Timor leaders and local groups are reinterpreting what resistance means, including taking a role in shaping the new state and fighting for new things like a better quality of life as Armindo Maia suggested (above). This reinterpretation is difficult work.

The history of the conflict also meant that simple operational questions carried more significant ethical messages than might be suspected at the outset in terms of who and what of the past was valued. A simple question like 'what language do you use for training and training materials' had significant implications for outsiders who were working in East Timor and with Timorese partners. While the majority of Timorese educated in schools during the twenty years preceding independence could speak Bahasa Indonesian, it was a language associated with the most recent occupiers. The language of Tetum was a common at-home language, viewed as distinctly Timorese, but limited in its vocabulary, and in part associated with the Catholic Church as it became more widely adopted when priests began to use it in liturgies. The language of Portuguese was the language that an older, elite generation learned in schools, and very familiar to those who led the resistance in exile, or who had *mestiços* ancestry. In peacebuilding initiatives, choosing to work in a particular language invoked a decision about which age group was valued as well as what social group was valued. Choosing to work in Tetum meant making a statement about supporting independence and valuing an at home language, despite its limitations. Choosing to work in Portuguese, valued a more elite language and favored leaders of the resistance and its Lusophone international support base. Working in Bahasa enabled clarity in terms of content for many, particularly the younger generation, but was also a reminder of Indonesian occupation. Working in English often occurred in international aid offices and favored those who had studied or been exiled in countries like Australia and favored Anglophone international partnerships. Each of these choices conveyed messages about who and what was valued to Timorese.

As peacebuilders we work where the past is often more than a shadow on the present. What does this past mean for the moral values held by stakeholders in the conflict? How has the conflict shaped the moral values of those around us? How do moral values shape how people respond to the conflict? In East Timor, the valorization of resistance was implicated in the reproduction of conflict, and the value itself was shaped by the many years of fighting power-over and domination. The conflict's historical context also affected the ethical messages of operational decisions. The past affected Timorese conceptions of good and right in multifaceted ways, to which peacebuilders needed to be attuned in order to do peacebuilding well.

LISTENING AND THINKING ABOUT MORAL VALUES WITH OTHERS

Even when we recognize that it is important to name and deliberate upon moral values, getting beyond our own filters and assumptions about right and good in order to identify values held by moral communities in conflict contexts is challenging. This suggests we need to pay attention to the process by which we surface moral values. Conflict analysis and mediation processes suggest a simple, helpful way forward: stakeholder analysis and consultation.

Stakeholder analysis and consultation are foundational for conflict resolution and transformation processes. Diverse points of view illuminate different aspects of a problem, present unique understandings of what is at stake in the conflict, draw out the power dynamics, and the historical context of the conflict. Stakeholder analysis adapted for ethics involves understanding moral value claims as well as the context in which they emerged, and how these values in turn shape the conflict context in which we work.

To move the idea of stakeholder consultation into an applied setting requires thinking about how and with whom to discuss moral values. There are a variety of people and groups to consider such as team members, an ombudsperson tasked with thinking about ethics and conflict for an organization as a whole, external colleagues who help think about professional ethics, partners, elders, community gatekeepers and the list goes on. Some colleagues I know have chosen to create accountability circles, a group of people who act as a sounding board and ask questions during periodic consultations in order to ensure they (the peacebuilders) are held accountable for their values and actions over time. In figure 3.1, there is an initial list of a variety of people and groups to consider consulting, in an effort to think broadly about who might have good insights and be helpful in widening out our process of ethical deliberation.

Considerations of how to navigate power disparities in our interactions with stakeholders in peacebuilding is a value-laden enterprise, as already noted. Do we value equality of participation? Do we think it is important to have marginalized populations have a greater say in decision-making? What do we do if others do not value the same level or type of participation as we do? To whose voices and advice are we really listening? Answering these questions can connect how we do our work with the ends we seek to achieve.

In my experience, identifying, sharing, and discussing values has opened up space for trust-building within peacebuilding initiatives. One organization I used to work for held periodic "justice lens" discussions with staff and partners. In these meetings we discussed the principles and underlying values, which were based upon Catholic social teaching and guided our work. As a non-Catholic, I facilitated discussions with partners and staff in Indonesia and Cambodia where the majority of participants were Muslim and Buddhist respectively. The conversations about values (like subsidiarity) and their fit (or not) with beliefs and traditions locally were fascinating and rich. They added depth to the relationships and led us to ask big, important questions about our work—such as, are we really working in a manner that reflects our values? If not, how do we change? Sharing perspectives on values helped to name troubling issues that weren't addressed elsewhere. For example, justice lens discussions in the Philippines moved the program to engage in

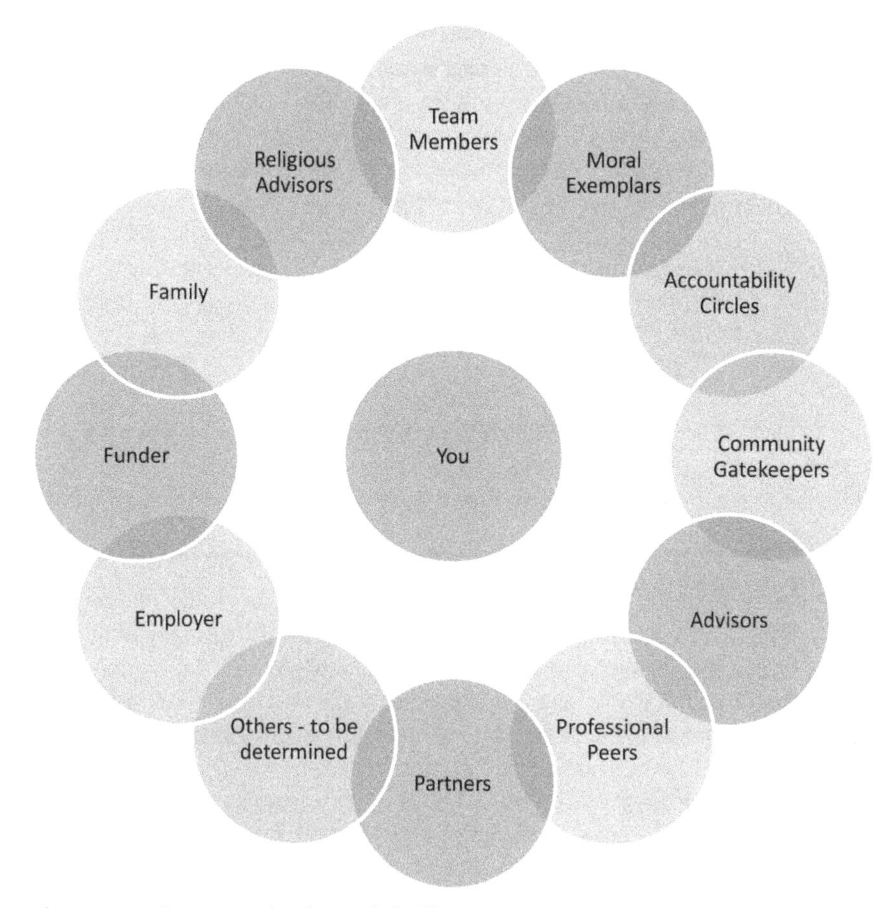

Figure 3.1. Some Moral Value Stakeholders

peacebuilding programming, rather than focusing solely on development in terms of agriculture and health. Program staff recognized that their projects and programs were not fully meeting the values they held and so reoriented in the mid-1990s.

In sum, to identify the moral values that are involved in our work and relevant to the issues we are facing, we start by watching for the value judgments that are made in terms of how we frame the problem(s) as well as what people hope to achieve (such as stability and order, relationships, and participation) and why stakeholders believe it is important to act. There are often multiple moral values involved when making a choice about any one issue, and therefore listening to a broad range of stakeholders is important. Identifying moral values is not difficult, but does take practice. Listening for and naming values that speak to legitimate needs and expectations involves opening up the space to listen to ourselves, to those around us, and to the value claims embedded in our operational language, how we define the problem, and why we do our work. It also involves paying attention to power and the historical context in which moral values are generated, and the ways in which these values inform our actions. We can do this on our own and with other people. Identifying moral values is one part of discerning how to act ethically. The next chapter identifies a set of four moral value claims which frequently appear in peacebuilding and can further help to focus discussions of moral values.

FOR FURTHER EXPLORATION

Here are some questions and activities that you can use to further think about issues raised in this chapter:

- Slavery is presented as an example of a shift in judgment about what was right versus wrong within a large population. What other issues are you aware of where people's moral judgments have shifted within your community? What do these shifts suggest for how we make judgments based upon our values today?
- In textbox 3.2, there are several quotes from sacred sources on the moral value of reciprocity. Are you aware of other examples of traditions that also hold the moral value of reciprocity? How, or in what ways, do you think that framing the moral value of reciprocity in a positive vein (e.g., do unto others) or negative way (e.g., do not do to others) affects actions?
- Below are two brief fictional scenarios that present moral dilemmas. Choose a location for the scenario (a location with which you are familiar) and adapt the information as needed. Then respond to the questions that follow.

  Scenario 1: You are a foreigner, an "expat," and a peacebuilder who is working as an advisor to a local organization; you arrived at your current placement about one year ago. You are affiliated with a donor organization although you do not directly control the budget. The local organization is doing great mediation work between guerilla fighters and local government units. Much of the success of this organization is attributed to the charismatic leader who is seen as a very effective mediator. You also find out that while the charismatic leader is a married man, he is using his status to pressure young women into what you consider to be inappropriate relationships with him. The family of one young woman in particular is outraged at his breach of moral conduct and has brought the issue to you, and is asking for your help. What are the values at stake here? How will you decide which values are most important? What role does power play here? How will you manage it? How might you respond?

Scenario 2: You are investigating human rights abuses as part of a transitional justice initiative within a country where a peace accord has been signed. You have been allowed into a rebel-controlled area with the understanding that you will interview adults about human rights violations they have experienced by the government during and prior to the conflict. Your overall project aims to explore the range of human rights violations perpetrated by any party. One informant tells you that she can get you interviews with some young children who were recruited by the rebel group at the age of ten to be military fighters—they are now between the ages of twelve and fourteen. She wants to know if you want to interview these children. What are the values at stake here? How will you decide which values are most important? What role does power play here? How will you manage it? How might you respond?

- With whom do you think it is important to consult regarding values and moral decisions in your work life? Why do you think it is important to consult with this person or set of people?
- What sources of moral authority are important within the context in which you live and work? What are some of the moral values embedded in those sources of authority? What kind of challenges arise when interpreting how moral values from this moral authority apply to a particular situation you are facing?
- In Sierra Leone, the international community supported Sierra Leone through the United Nations Peacebuilding Fund to develop various aspects of its liberal democracy, including supporting elections and a judiciary system that fits international rule of law standards.[11] UN-sponsored peacebuilding activities tended to be geared toward legal, economic, and political development and, to a lesser extent, social capital development. In contrast, grassroots peacebuilding tended to work directly with those affected by conflict, designing and leading reconciliation processes. Fambul tok is one example of a grassroots reconciliation initiative within Sierra Leone that focused on communities leading a process of restoring relationships between victims and perpetrators of violence in their midst. This approach drew on Sierra Leonean culture and tradition and brought those, even those who had committed atrocities, back into society and community. What moral values are being invoked in these

choices? How might social location and power affect the moral values being foregrounded?

NOTES

1. The United Nations Peacebuilding Commission Burundi Configuration statement is available on the UN website at: http://www.un.org/en/peacebuilding/doc_burundi.shtml.

2. The Charter of the United Nations was initially drafted by the Allied powers during World War II; it was signed by fifty member states on June 26, 1945, officially coming into force in October of that same year, and while there have been some amendments to the original charter, the last amendment came into force in 1973. The full charter as well as an introduction to the document are available online at: http://www.un.org/en/documents/charter/index.shtml. For an excellent background on UN peacekeeping and the move to peacebuilding, see Alex Bellamy and Paul D. Williams, *Understanding Peacekeeping* (second edition, Malden, MA: Polity Press, 2010). For an exploration of the relationship between peacebuilding and statebuilding, see Charles T. Call's edited book with Vanessa Wyth, *Building States to Build Peace* (Boulder, CO: Lynne Rienner Publishers, Inc., 2008), or the section on the infrastructure of peacebuilding in Roger Mac Ginty's edited book, *Routledge Handbook of Peacebuilding* (New York: Routledge, 2013).

3. Richard Rorty explores the question of moral community in "Who Are We? Moral Universalism and Economic Triage" (*Diogenes,* 173(44):5–15, 1996). Tim Murithi's reflection on the relationship between ethics, peacebuilding, and moral community appear in his book *The Ethics of Peacebuilding* (Edinburgh: Edinburgh University Press, 2009).

4. The quotes on reciprocity come from Jeffrey Wattles, *The Golden Rule* (New York: Oxford University Press, 1996). Further exploration of the ethic of reciprocity from various religious perspectives is available in Jacob Neusner and Bruce Chilton's edited volume, *The Golden Rule: The Ethics of Reciprocity in World Religions* (New York: Continuum International Publishing Group, 2009).

5. For an introductory exploration of moral reasoning in Judaism, Islam, and Christianity, see Charles Mathewes's *Understanding Religious Ethics* (West Sussex: Wiley-Blackwell, 2010).

6. In the discussion of power, the five dimensions of power referred to as part of the definition of power come from John French and Bertram Raven's 1959 chapter titled "The Bases of Social Power" (in *Studies in Social Power*, edited by D. Cartwright; Ann Arbor, MI: University of Michigan, Institute for Social Research, pp. 150–67). Herbert Kelman and Donald Warwick wrote about the importance of looking at power in conflict resolution in what is considered a classic piece titled "The Ethics of Social Intervention: Goals, Means, and Consequences" (in *The Ethics of Social Intervention*, edited by Gordon Bermant, Herbert C. Kelman, and Donald P. Warwick; Washington, DC: Hemisphere Publishing Corporation, 1978, pp. 3–33). In

the same volume, you can also read Jim Laue and Gerald Cormick's classic article "The Ethics of Intervention in Community Disputes" which draws out issues of power and the ethical problem of neutrality in mediation work (*The Ethics of Social Intervention,* 1978, pp. 205–32).

7. The United Nations Declaration on the Rights of Indigenous Peoples is available online at: http://www.un.org/esa/socdev/unpfii/documents/DRIPS_en.pdf.

8. John Calhoun's speech is available online at: http://teachingamericanhistory.org/library/document/slavery-a-positive-good/.

9. The quote from Angelina Grimké's "Appeal to the Christian Women of the South" comes from *Walden and Civil Disobedience,* edited by Paul Lauter (New York: Houghton Mifflin Company, 2000, pp. 267–86); a further example from Grimké is available in Karlyn Kohrs Campbell, Susan Schultz Huxman, and Thomas Burkholder's *The Rhetorical Act: Thinking, Speaking and Writing Critically* (fifth edition, Stamford, CT: Cengage Learning, 2014, pp. 212–16). Frederick Douglass' *Narrative of the Life of Frederick Douglass, an American Slave* (New York: Signet Books, 2005) provides his compelling story and was a foundational text for the abolitionist movement. For a biography and exploration of Sojourner Truth, see Nell Irvin Painter's *Sojourner Truth, A Life, A Symbol* (New York: W. W. Norton, 1997). For an extensive history of the slave trade and economic production, see David Brion Davis's *Inhuman Bondage: The Rise and Fall of Slavery in the New World* (New York: Oxford University Press, 2006). The selection from Miguel De La Torre comes from his edited volume *Ethics: A Liberative Approach* (Minneapolis: Fortress Press, 2013).

10. A detailed description of the events of May and June 2006 are reported in International Crisis Group's "Resolving Timor-Leste's Crisis" (Jakarta/Brussels: International Crisis Group, 2006). The case study on East Timor draws on Sara Niner's "Martyrs, Heroes and Warriors: the Leadership of East Timor" (pp. 113–28) and Michael Leach's "History Teaching: Challenges and Alternatives" (pp. 193–207) in Damien Kingsbury and Michael Leach (eds.), *East Timor: Beyond Independence* (Victoria: Monash University Press, 2007), as well as Donísio da Costa Babo Soares's doctoral dissertation *Branching from the Trunk: East Timorese Perceptions of Nationalism in Transition* (Australia National University, 2003). The full constitution of East Timor is available in English from the government's website at: http://timor-leste.gov.tl/wp-content/uploads/2010/03/Constitution_RDTL_ENG.pdf.

11. For an overview of the conflict and peacebuilding in Sierra Leone, see the Conciliation Resources publication *Accord,* issue 9, *Paying the Price: The Sierra Leonean Peace Process* (London; Conciliation Resources, 2000), and issue 23, *Accord: Consolidating Peace Liberia and Sierra Leone* (London; Conciliation Resources, 2013). For a helpful critical perspective on issues related to truth-telling and reconciliation in Sierra Leone, see Rosalind Shaw's report "Rethinking Truth and Reconciliation Commissions: Lessons from Sierra Leone" (Washington, DC: United States Institute of Peace, 2005). For more on the process of Fambul Tok, I recommend viewing the documentary *Fambul Tok* (directed by Sara Terry and produced by Rory Kennedy and Libby Hoffman; New York: First Run Features, 2011).

4

Thinking Carefully

How Moral Theories Help

MORAL THEORIES—WHAT THEY OFFER

This chapter presents a number of moral theory perspectives to consider in the course of peacebuilding work. Four moral values are examined through the lenses of five moral theory perspectives (the theories are listed in parentheses): (1) ends (consequentialism), (2) duties (deontology also known as duty-based ethics), (3) relationality (care and Ubuntu), and (4) character (virtue). Yet there is a fundamental question to be asked before exploring these moral value perspectives: Why use moral theories to help us think and act ethically?

Lying behind this question is the suggestion that we can think through moral problems well enough without other formal inputs. There is merit in this argument as these theories were themselves products of people thinking carefully and systematically through moral problems and about moral values. Further, moral theories are not substitutes for thinking carefully, which means we still must engage in open and careful thinking *even* when using them.

So, what use are moral theories? Their worth rests in the values they focus on and the structure they provide (see textbox 4.1). They help to systematically reason through the quagmire of questions that arise when thinking about what is good or right in order to get to ethical action. Moral theories offer us a logical scaffolding for thinking about an issue or problem, which—like temporary scaffolding of wood and metal put up when walls are built or repaired—enables us to think about a problem from a consistent, stable perspective. A moral theory allows us to focus on a set of concerns around a particular moral value or set of values, and not worry about other potentially destabilizing things. For example, when we use consequentialist moral theory, we ask a constrained set of questions from a stable values position *vis-à-vis* "ends." In this way, moral theories draw specific problems to our attention and help us analyze them more quickly than we might otherwise. Moral theories are helpful in identifying moral values that speak to legitimate needs and expectations held in common within a moral community, and which go beyond individual self-interest or egoism.

Philosophers and ethicists tend to analyze contemporary moral issues from the perspective of one moral theory. This sometimes translates into peacebuilding analysis when one moral theory perspective is repeatedly drawn upon by peacebuilders. For example, there is a consistent argument that we should do no harm in development and peacebuilding work. This argument centers on assessing the outcomes of our work and therefore is consistently made from the perspective of consequentialist moral theory. We frequently see consequentialism in peacebuilding, especially where our concept of good peacebuilding is yoked to impact in which good ends are understood to be those effects that reach the greatest number of people. It is not, however, the only way to understand *good* nor is it the only moral theory or moral value relevant to peacebuilding. There is something to be gained by thinking about moral theories in the plural.

James Sterba, a contemporary ethicist, suggests we approach different moral theory traditions collaboratively. Rather than arguing about which moral theory is best, we can use a variety of moral theories together to ponder a concern and find points of consensus as well as divergence. In this chapter there are five moral theories that center on four moral values. The scaffolding of these moral theories help to think through our moral problems from different vantage points, including thinking about ourselves as peacebuilders,

TEXTBOX 4.1. SUMMARY: HOW MORAL THEORIES CAN HELP US

Moral theories:

- Focus on key aspects of moral problems;
- Consider individuals and larger moral communities;
- Draw out the complexity of a problem from a moral value perspective;
- Provide us with scaffolding for our thinking (which can help us think through a problem faster);
- Can be used collaboratively; and
- Provide guidance for action.

how we do our work, how we relate to one another, and for what ends. In this way, collectively, these moral theories speak to central claims of good and right in peacebuilding today; claims which are used both by state-level peacebuilding actors as well as grassroots-level peacebuilding actors, albeit with different emphases.

My contention that these five moral theories (consequentialism, deontology, virtue, care, and Ubuntu), offer a diverse set of lenses to weigh and assess peacebuilding also requires scrutiny. Each moral theory emerged at a particular place and time, although they have been modified over time. As the previous chapter discussed, our moral value perspectives reflect the social context in which we live. How then can these five theories be helpful for peacebuilders who work in very diverse contexts? In places where moral values may be understood or enacted differently? And, when values themselves might be part of the conflict?

The first two moral theories that follow, consequentialism and deontology (or duty-based ethics), emerged largely out of Enlightenment thinking in Europe. Therefore, these two moral theories reflect similar assumptions in terms of valuing individuals as possessing equal moral worth, valuing rationality, and claiming universal application. While consequentialism and Kantian-based moral thinking were seen to be radical when they were produced, they are also critiqued by current scholars and activists as representing values that reinforce patterns of power and privilege in today's international system (see, for example, Miguel De La Torre's quote in textbox 3.4 in the previous chapter).

Despite such critiques, consequentialism and duty-based moral thinking are both frequently used in judgments by actors in large-scale peacebuilding institutions, such as the United Nations, in part because they reflect the moral values behind the institutions when they were established, and in part because they are argued to be universal. Human rights law, which is not itself a moral theory (see textbox 4.2), was derived in part from these two traditions. Consequentialism and duty-based moral theories are therefore worth considering because they bring to the fore dominant concerns in contemporary, large-scale peacebuilding, consider dimensions of equality as a component of justice, and help us focus on the ends that we pursue as well as our duties to one another as peacebuilders.

The third moral theory explored in this chapter focuses on our moral character as peacebuilders. Modern virtue ethics, which is a variation of classic virtue ethics, centers its understanding of what constitutes the good and right on the self and a life well-lived within moral communities based on moral character. Virtues (excellence of character) brings into focus ourselves as peacebuilders and the intimate connection between our ways of being and embodying morality, which inherently contributes to collective flourishing.

TEXTBOX 4.2. WHITHER HUMAN RIGHTS?

In today's news headlines, human rights often are touted as the standard by which we should judge the action of companies, nations, and neighbors. Naming and shaming human rights violators can be an advocacy strategy to pressure actors to change their ways. In my focus on moral theories I am not using human rights as a term, and some are likely asking "why not?"

Some moral theories do use rights language. People can possess positive rights as an entitlement to something, which is then connected to duties by others to respect those rights; or people can possess negative rights, which requires others to refrain from actions. Moral rights, however, are not the same as legal rights. Legal human rights are based upon a legal system, statute, or convention. The Universal Declaration of Human Rights institutionalized human rights in 1948 as part of the United Nations system, in good measure drawing on Natural Law and contractualism. Natural Law suggests we all possess innate and inalienable rights based on human nature, and contractualism suggests that the content of these rights are negotiated in social contracts, such as a constitution in which citizens are recognized as all possessing the right to life, liberty, and security—and often property is added to this list. Human rights claims reflect a particular understanding of moral values that are predicated on moral theory but codified into legal frameworks. Moral rights, in contrast, are independent of legal systems.

Consequentialism and Kantian duty-based ethics, explored later, both recognize rights. Yet, the moral foundation of these theories centers on moral valuing of good ends or duties to do right. I use a focus on moral values to understand and promote ethics in peacebuilding because we are looking to uncover, weigh, and deliberate upon multiple moral values that are involved in our work which occurs at the intersection of divided moral communities in which legal systems are often not operational or are themselves enmeshed in the conflict. This is not to say that human rights are not useful or important concepts (they are); however, our moral thinking needs to go beyond and deeper than a human rights-based framework to be ethical.

Two moral theory perspectives together view relationality as a moral good. These are care and Ubuntu, also referred to as ethics of care and Ubuntu ethics. They both suggest to us an alternative worldview of ethics wherein our interconnections are valued at the forefront of our moral considerations, as opposed to making autonomous moral decisions as distanced individuals. Here, responsiveness and interconnections are foregrounded in analysis.

Modern virtues theory, care, and Ubuntu enable us to be context-responsive when thinking about moral values while still providing a central claim. The content of these moral theories becomes evident only when thinking about morality that is embedded within relationships and the particularities of the moral communities with which we work. Who we are as peacebuilders in a community, how we act, and how we relate to those around us are of vital concern to peacebuilders in the day-to-day operations of peacebuilding. These considerations, and critiques of the lack thereof, often mark the complaints of grassroots peacebuilders and local communities against international peacebuilders (e.g., that foreign peacebuilders are distanced, think they know what is right, are unaware of local norms and insult locals, corrupt local youth and engage in immoral acts). Relationality and virtue are of central concern to peacebuilders in applied work and speak to the values we ourselves enact and live out.

Together then these five moral theories (consequentialism, duty-based ethics, virtue ethics, ethics of care, and Ubuntu ethics) offer us ways of thinking about ethics from different perspectives which cover a broad range of concerns and critiques in current peacebuilding interventions. While they do not represent all possible moral values, they do speak to central values concerns evident in peacebuilding practice today by grassroots peacebuilders as well as by international peacebuilders. In what follows, each theory is briefly summarized in order to draw attention to the central value-focus of the theory and then applied. This means I do not explore the variations in each moral theory family, nor the full breadth and range of moral thinking in each perspective. Additional resources are listed in the Notes section for those interested in reading more deeply about the rich moral theory traditions.[1]

CONSEQUENCES

Consequentialist ethics are familiar to many of us. From a consequentialist perspective, the rightness of an action is determined by whether it helps bring about a better outcome than its alternatives. A foundation of consequentialism was utilitarian thinking, which originally was articulated by Jeremy Bentham and his famous student John Stuart Mill. For Bentham, an act was morally right if and only if it maximized the good, and here "good" was equated with the greatest happiness for the most number of people. To determine if an act was morally right there was a "felicitous calculation" where the amount of good generated by an action was calculated, and the amount of bad generated by an action was also calculated and subtracted from the good. The right action was that which produced the greater net amount of good as compared to any alternative action one might take on the same occasion (or at least as good as any other course of action one might take).

Notice in this line of thinking the moral quality of an action is determined based upon the effects of that action. An act is not good or bad in and of itself, but rather it is good or bad based upon whether it instrumentally produces the greatest outcome: if it maximizes happiness. For example, lying is not intrinsically wrong but it is wrong if it produces an outcome that does not maximize the good (understood as happiness).

There are many variations of consequentialism, which allows for great moral debate. For example, you can think of the outcomes of specific acts (e.g., one instance of lying) or more broadly in terms of the outcomes from broader rules (e.g., a rule against lying) in determining consequences. In both approaches, the consequences of either the act or the rule are compared, so that the rightness or wrongness of an action or rule depends upon how much good it procures in comparison to any other actions or rules. This approach sounds very familiar in that it's similar to cost-benefit calculations many make, particularly in business settings. Bentham and Mill were considered radical British political reformers when they proposed consequentialism because they argued that, in this comparative process, it didn't matter *who* was affected (whose happiness counted), rather the consequences for everyone were to be considered equally regardless of social and economic status—whether one was a landless peasant or a land-holding lord. The equality of application in a hierarchical context was radical.

Consequentialism is quite evident in peacebuilding, particularly in outcome evaluations when people are asking questions like: Was this program doing the right things to produce the greatest contribution to peace? Or, did the benefits of this intervention outweigh the harms? Consequentialism is also evident in program planning because one aspect of consequentialist analysis is to assess probable outcomes—what is likely to happen when we pursue this action? What is likely to happen if we pursued another line of action?

The idea that we are looking for the greatest positive consequences or greatest good for the most people is beguilingly simple. Understanding what constitutes the good, and how we might compare it to alternative courses of action, is more challenging than it looks. If peacebuilding evaluation is any indication, while people resonate with the call to be effective and produce the greatest outcomes, it is a significant challenge to assess whether or not our work actually produced the best effects, and if it produced any verifiable effects at all. There are a significant number of variables to consider. To assess consequences, you need to make probability-based guesses about intended and unintended effects that might happen in different scenarios. This means generating realistic assessments and due diligence to gather as much information as possible in order to make an informed decision. Even with extensive information about choices, there will be uncertainties in calculating benefits and harms, especially in complex systems.

In sum, though it may be difficult to measure, consequentialist moral theory helps us to focus on the intended and unintended effects of our work. We need to make reasonable assessments of the likely effects of our actions when assessing whether or not we are doing the right things and contributing to what is just and good. Key questions one asks when pursuing this line of moral thinking are: What good will realistically come out of this initiative (intended and unintended)? What harms (or bad) will realistically result from this initiative (intended and unintended)? Can I mitigate the harms? Which action or sets of actions that we are proposing in our peacebuilding efforts will produce the greatest good overall? How do the outcomes of the possible actions compare? These key questions are summarized in textbox 4.3 and help to concentrate on the ends or effects of our work.

TEXTBOX 4.3. CONSEQUENCES: KEY QUESTIONS

What good will come from this action? (Intended and unintended)

What harms will come from this action? (Intended and unintended)

Will this action produce the best consequences overall?

Consequentialism applied. A short example can help clarify what a focus on consequences brings to applied ethics in peacebuilding. This example focuses on the decision of a local peacebuilding organization located in Jos, Nigeria, and whether or not to share information from a conflict analysis with security sector actors or the public. The example is fictional although it draws on elements of the context and challenges that peacebuilders confront in Jos in order to explore how the moral theory applies.

Jos is the capital of Plateau State and has experienced several cycles of violence since 1999. While large-scale violence has been limited since 2010, there have been a number of bombings attributed to the group Boko Haram which have taken numerous lives and threatened stability and relationships in the area. The picture on the cover of this book captures an image of Jos taken in an area that has been slower to recover from the violence of 2010; however, in the background of the picture you can see signs of recovery and life—active peacebuilding in Jos has helped mitigate escalating violence despite recent bombings. Yet Jos has experienced divisions in its population which persist, there is a sizable youth population that has been vulnerable to manipulation by political leaders for personal gain and a number of deeply-seated contentious issues (see resources in the Notes section for greater detail). Our illustrative example takes place in this context.

A local organization has engaged in careful conflict analysis with various community stakeholders and has developed a complex picture of the grievances and issues that matter for a diverse set of stakeholders. This conflict analysis includes view points from a range of groups that are in opposing political parties and, within it, particular issues are named and individuals and groups implicated as participating in or leading the violence. The organization has been asked by security forces to share the conflict analysis with them. The ethical question before the organization then is whether or not to share their conflict analysis with the security forces or, even more broadly, with the public (e.g., by posting it online).

Assessing the request from a consequentialist perspective brings the ends into focus. Members of the organization will ask: What good will come from this action? For example, police and security actors might be better positioned to prevent violence and promote law and order if they are better informed about the grievances as well as the stakeholders and issues in the conflict. If the conflict analysis information is shared publicly, then everyone in the community will have equal access to the information, which might reduce the use of inflammatory rumors. Making the conflict analysis public would also allow other peacebuilding organizations to benefit from the analysis, and that could be used to improve efforts overall in the area—particularly if groups can coordinate together and address the full range of actors and concerns. Cumulatively, these are very good outcomes, which could increase the overall security situation in Jos, and improve peacebuilding initiatives' abilities to address the full range of issues and actors.

The next consequentialist question is what harms might occur because of this action. One level of harms would be to individuals who shared information in the conflict analysis, which was confidential. While information is not directly attributed, it might nevertheless be "decoded" and used in retributive violence against parties—targeting those with grievances or those who had named others as instigating violence. This targeting might well be done extra-judiciously. It would also be important to consider harms to the organization itself: Would the act of sharing undermine their ability to be a trusted actor and build trust in the community? There are also potential harms to the larger community. Political parties, security forces, or extremists might exploit this knowledge for their own gain by playing on constituent fears, by strategically maneuvering to undermine other groups' concerns, or creating new alliances with groups with whom they were previously not connected.

In thinking through harms, we consider probabilities and whether or not there are ways to mitigate the harms. The good outcomes and the possible harms of different courses of action are then weighed against each other. A consequentialist perspective demands we choose the course of action that will yield the overall greatest good (or at least as good an outcome as any other course of action) based on our rational calculation. In looking at the above analysis, we may decide that sharing the information broadly will produce the greatest general good for the overall population because more people will have access to the information, thereby producing better focused peacebuilding. Sharing the analysis will enhance security forces' ability to ensure order *if* we also undertake measures at the same time to ensure the military and police do not over-step their authority, and minimize extrajudicial activities. We may also need to work to improve the fairness of the legal system to improve its functioning. The overall good of stability for everyone living in Jos is assessed to be at least as good an outcome as any other course of action. Note, however, that some harms are permissible in the calculation. So it is acceptable if one or two people are targets of attack because information is shared publicly, because the harms to one or two people do not outweigh the overall benefits. It also is acceptable to have some manipulation of information by political leaders if the overall good is determined to be better than (or at least as good as) other courses of action.

DUTIES

Duty-based ethics are often called deontological ethics, derived from the Greek words *deon* for duty and *logos* for the science or study thereof. The central claim is that some actions are simply good in and of themselves, regardless of the outcomes. In duty-based ethics, the emphasis is on discovering and then performing actions (duties) that are intrinsically good. For example, you need to determine if telling the truth is an intrinsically good action and if it is, then you are obligated to tell the truth regardless of the consequences (e.g., one must tell the truth even if telling a lie might protect some innocent child's life). In duty-based reasoning, we think through principles or rules in advance, which we are then morally obliged to follow.

Immanuel Kant, the foremost thinker of duty-based ethics, was an eighteenth century German philosopher who argued that moral action was guided by moral (practical) reason and by pragmatic principles that were designed to help people make judgments and resolve problems. Kant identified two types of duties for action called imperatives, which were intrinsically good or right actions: hypothetical imperatives and categorical imperatives. Hypothetical imperatives were practical things that one chose to do to accomplish some prudent end. For example, exercising your body regularly to achieve good health, or coordinating interventions to achieve synchronous peacebuilding, are practical things that each of us can do to accomplish the prudent end that serves our interests. However, these are not universal moral requirements from Kant's perspective. They are good, and so it is good if we follow them, but we are not morally *obliged* to follow them.

In contrast, we are morally required to follow categorical imperatives. Categorical imperatives refer to actions required of everyone, unconditionally, in order to act in a moral manner. Kant's two tests of whether something was a categorical imperative involved whether or not you could imagine it being applied universally without any contradictions in the logic, and whether or not it could be done. For example, consider my first example of exercise. If we want to consider whether regular physical exercise is a universal imperative, we have to consider whether or not we can think of everyone doing it universally. Immediately we realize that if people are injured, ill, or immobile then they cannot reasonably be asked to exercise regularly and so it fails to be something we can imagine applying universally as a moral requirement. Kant offered several versions of his categorical imperative, and the one most frequently referred to today is the humanity imperative: always treat people as ends and never simply as means to an end (very similar to the value of reciprocity discussed in chapter three).

Current duty-based ethics go beyond Kant's original formulations and yet are consistently marked by the idea of universal requirements to follow principles or rules, and constraints for the protection of people. The word universal here means that the principle or imperative applies to everyone equally regardless of culture and context—culture and context are irrelevant from this perspective. Principles or rules guide our action through the articulation of constraints on what we do. Duties may also be framed as rights and responsibilities. For example, we have a duty to treat all humans as equal and as bearers of the same rights. In development work, intriguingly, the consequentialist injunction of "do no harm" has now become a duty that is expected to be upheld by all aid workers (we have a duty to follow this rule, which converges with rule utilitarianism). Other duties with which we are familiar in peacebuilding work are the right to human security and the responsibility to protect human security.

Many duty-based ethicists diverge from Kant today by arguing that at some point after we have acted we can choose to decline to do more. The argument is that there are limits to our duties and, while we may admire those who make great additional sacrifices, we ourselves are not obligated to do so. For example, if you act to preserve someone's life once, you do not need to continue to act in order to preserve that life if it comes at a great cost to yourself. This seems particularly important in peacebuilding when peacebuilders may be unaware of their own trauma and continue to act based upon the belief that it is their duty to help others even as they are being damaged in the process.

There are also others who look at duties as moral "oughts," which include duties that we ought to do generally on the face of it, called *prima facie duties*, but can be over-ridden by other moral duties if something changes significantly and a competing duty comes to the fore. For example, if a life-threatening accident occurs in front of you, it takes precedence over running a peacebuilding training workshop; the priority is to respond to the immediate situation before responding to the other duty, which would have been prioritized in regular circumstances. Moral judgment is then needed to decide which duties are more important at a given moment in time.

Duties themselves, however, are not simply things you decide are right in a given moment nor right because someone in greater authority told you to do something. Duties are moral "oughts" that need to be carefully reasoned, and once principles are identified, reasoning is needed again to identify how to apply the principles in the specific context in which one finds oneself. Duty-based moral theory focuses on the requirements that we have to treat people equally and justly. It also involves reasoning and considering what is right—preferably under conditions of equity and liberty. When we look at our peacebuilding decisions from a duty-based perspective, we ask questions that focus on how we are acting vis-à-vis our universal obligations (also listed in textbox 4.4): Are we upholding our obligations? Are we treating people as ends and not merely as means? Are we treating people as possessing equal moral rights? Are these moral obligations reasonable and ones to which rational individuals, under conditions of freedom and equity, consent? Through these questions, we assess our own consistency and the justness of our application of ideas within and across our peacebuilding initiatives.

Duties applied. To apply duty-based analysis to the moral challenge of whether or not to share a detailed conflict analysis publicly and with security forces in Jos shifts our understanding of what matters from the preceding

TEXTBOX 4.4. DUTIES: KEY QUESTIONS

What are the moral obligations and responsibilities that are required of everyone (universal)? Am I (are we) following our moral obligations?

Am I (are we) treating people as ends in and of themselves or as means to an end? Are we treating everyone as having equal moral claims (rights)?

Are these moral obligations reasonable? (Would rational individuals under conditions of liberty and equity consent?)

consequentialist application. A duty-based perspective focuses us on the right thing to do because of its intrinsic good regardless of consequences. Of central concern is the value of people, and to ensure that people are always treated as ends and never as a means to an end. For the organization, to apply the categorical imperative they have to treat all those who engaged in the conflict analysis (as well as the community) as ends in and of themselves, and not just sources to produce a thorough analysis or some overall calculation of good for everyone. The organization therefore needs to act in ways that ensure stakeholders and other community members are not used as means. For example, the organization might decide to ask people who participated in the conflict analysis if they consent to the information being shared publicly through a careful and rational deliberative process. If participants whose lives may be at risk because of information shared in the conflict analysis say no, then the organization is obliged to not share it. The organization may also recognize their duty to protect community members from harm (which they reason is something people under conditions of freedom and equity would agree with), and decide not to share the conflict analysis even without conferring with stakeholders. These obligations sound reasonable as it does not impose undue duress on the organization or people within it or outside of it. The decision might therefore be made to not share the conflict analysis from a duty-based perspective to fully respect obligations to stakeholders. The organization might choose to engage on conflict issues some other way to also respond to other persons in the community, but protect the information gathered from their conflict analysis.

VIRTUES

Virtue thinking, also called virtue ethics, offers a third prominent moral theory. This line of analysis emphasizes the virtuous individual and his or her character, dispositions, and motivations. The focus of moral analysis is on one's character and personal quality. A virtuous life is a life that is well-lived and contributes to collective flourishing, which in Greek is referred to as *eudemonia.* In *eudemonia,* flourishing is sometimes called happiness or living well collectively. From this perspective, you do not do good because you have to (which would be one's duty) or because of the outcomes that your actions will produce (which would be consequentialist), but you do good because you *are* good and embody excellence of character. A virtuous person lives a good life, one that is morally admirable and responds to the demands of the world. From this perspective, your emotional reactions, choices, values, desires, perceptions, expectations, interests and sensibilities all reflect the virtues you possess. If you know what is truly worthwhile and truly important you will know how to live well and achieve eudemonia. We can understand *eudemonia* (flourishing) as a good end that is constituted through our living well.

Aristotle's argument for virtue ethics emerged in the late classical period of Greece. The classical period was marked by significant chaos and war, with Philip the Macedonian king defeating the Greeks at the Battle of Chaeronea in 338 BC. In this context of division, the quest for reason and order provided a unifying ideal in Greek literature and philosophy. The idea was that existence was ordered, and that human ability and reason could create a balanced society. To achieve this, the aim of life should be balance, and everything in proportion. For Aristotle, virtues reflected balance and one sought to live out a golden mean of one's virtues, while excess or deficit of a virtue produced vice (e.g., too much courage is rashness or foolhardiness, too little courage is cowardice, and the golden mean is courage). Aristotle developed an extensive list of virtues. Other classic Greek philosophers identified four virtues: temperance, prudence, courage, and justice.

Basing morality on personal character traits is not unique to the ancient Greeks, although the ancient Greek view strongly influenced Christian perspectives on virtues and western philosophy. Importantly, other ancient traditions, such as Confuscianism, Hinduism, and Buddhism, also emphasize personal virtues and character development. They draw to the fore distinctive moral characteristics such as compassion, mindfulness, non-attachment, and nonviolence, offering a different set of virtues than the classic Greek list of virtues.

Virtue ethics was revived in Western philosophy in the 1980s. Rather than identifying a pre-existing set of virtues, Alasdair MacIntyre argued we can identify what is virtuous through the narratives of our society; we can look at what is valued and sought after as morally good in the way we speak and write about what constitutes a life well-lived in communities to identify what is virtuous. Thus, rather than using pre-defined categories of virtue, we can identify virtues by listening to and engaging with people to understand what a life well-lived means in the specific context in which we are living and working. We can also think about our own life as part of a larger story that existed before we entered into it, and which will continue on after we exit; we are a small part of a larger story of a quest for the good life. Our story is therefore part of a narrative quest within larger moral communities. We identify virtues and virtuous actions within a shared moral community, which requires moral discernment and practical wisdom.[2]

It may be helpful to note that virtue ethicists don't assume that people are automatically virtuous. We can develop our virtues with experience and education. Virtues are necessarily accompanied by "practical wisdom" or *phronesis,* to ensure that a specific character trait doesn't become a flaw. Practical wisdom requires the capacity to recognize, in a given situation, the features that are morally salient and more important to consider. For example, practical wisdom will help you to discern when it is morally good to conceal a hurtful truth from a friend, or when it is morally good for that friend to hear the hurtful truth in order to benefit them. This type of practical wisdom develops over time through experience, engagement with others within the moral community, and by watching virtuous individuals.

Virtue ethics enables us to ask questions about ourselves, our character traits and dispositions as peacebuilders, and to respect the context in which we work. Virtues, drawing on modern virtue ethics, do not involve a preconstituted list of virtues. Modern virtue ethics require listening for what is understood to be virtuous in the stories and practices of a community. The purpose of listening is not a greater end per se, but of becoming more virtuous oneself. Deciding what to do requires practical wisdom, which can be cultivated through experience and education but is not something that is self-evident nor prescribed by a rule or principle. We can ask questions about what is virtuous in a given setting, as well as in ourselves and our ability to live out a morally laudable life in our work. We can look for exemplars and assess their example. Key questions to help think about virtue ethics are summarized in textbox 4.5. This perspective enables us to bring who we are and what motivates us as we assess what is ethical within peacebuilding.

Virtues applied. Applying virtues ethics in practice is quite different than the first two moral theories. Rather than focusing on external calculations, the

TEXTBOX 4.5. VIRTUES: KEY QUESTIONS

What is considered virtuous in this context? Am I upholding these virtues?

Am I living a life well-lived?

What would a virtuous person do in this situation?

focus is on the "I" as a peacebuilder and what it means for me to live well within the context in which I am living and working. It involves prudential thinking about the self as part of a larger quest for collective flourishing. One component of this thinking involves contemplating what is virtuous for me and embodies living a well-lived, excellent life in Jos (to continue with that example), which contributes to collective flourishing. Some virtues may be those distilled in conversation with residents and moral exemplars of Jos. I also bring into this context my profession as a peacebuilder, which has its own set of virtues or characteristics integral to this vocation, such as being respectful, possessing integrity, and compassion.

In these deliberations, the context and the moral community's narrative matters. From a modern virtues perspective, the context shapes our narratives, our understanding of what a life-well lived means, and what a quest for the good life and flourishing looks like. My first step, therefore, is to listen for and think about what characteristics are integral to living a good life—one marked by moral excellence of character (which is different than a life of wealth and monetary gain)—here and as a peacebuilder. To do this, I may consult with moral exemplars or elders as well as respected peacebuilding colleagues. I look to great moral exemplars in Jos, from the stories that people tell as well as the people I know. I will also need the wisdom (*phronesis*) to discern what action to take—drawing on my past experience as well as moral education that I've received and thinking about what my courageous exemplars would do in this situation.

Perhaps, in looking at exemplar peacebuilders in Jos, the characteristics of courage as well as trustworthiness and solidarity (acting in a way that mutually supports groups) come to the fore. I enact these virtues and in doing so I live a well-lived life and contribute to flourishing in Jos. In enacting the virtues myself, I discern ways to act that enable me to retain my trustworthiness as a peacebuilder with those in the community, as well as have the courage to connect with diverse groups without divulging information that will jeopardize lives or relationships. In the end, I have not shared the information but I have built up capacities to connect and engage in conversations that will produce similar knowledge. Notice that in the analysis it is awkward to predict action from a virtue ethics perspective outside of how to think about character and choices and building moral character. The action is a process of moral discernment that requires listening to those around oneself, and living out virtues that contribute to flourishing.

RELATIONSHIPS: CARE AND UBUNTU

A challenge for us in peace and conflict work is to think ethically about relationships. Relationships are central in peacebuilding because of the fissures and fractures in social relationships as well as the wide variety of political, social, and legal systems in place (or not in place) within settings of conflict. Dealing with relationships and relationality tends to recede into the background in the previous three moral theory perspectives as we discern a good way to be, the right thing to do, or a good outcome. Duty-based and consequentialist ethics in particular rely upon approaching ethics from a distanced perspective, where one reasons "behind a veil" as John Rawls framed it—distancing oneself emotionally in deliberation. One assesses the right thing to do without thinking about specific relationships that might connect people, nor knowing how the decision will affect you—which is why Rawls used the phrase "behind a veil." This approach means that considerations of equity are brought front and center; however, it also means considerations of relationships, and recognizing how our connections to others are part of our moral life, are less obvious.

Throughout life we live in relationship with others; sometimes intimately with parents, spouses, and children, and at other times at a distance. With relationships come emotional commitments, which we can understand as a source for moral thinking and action rather than a threat—particularly since emotions often motivate us to persist long after our intellectual commitments fade or change. Two lines of moral thinking help bring relationships and interconnectedness to the fore: care and Ubuntu. This section focuses on these two moral theory perspectives, although there are other relational moral theories such as H. Richard Niebuhr's ethics of responsibility, which also begins with an understanding that humans respond to other influences (individuals, communities, God, and so forth). In all of these approaches, we are understood not to be autonomous moral agents but rather people who are in relationship with others, and we start moral questioning by asking what is occurring within a given context rather than with considerations of duty or ends.

Care. The ethics of care emerges from feminist thinking about ethics. Here there is an emphasis on viewing responsiveness within relationships as a moral good. From an ethics of care standpoint, morality requires being responsive to others' needs, which might include their material needs, psychological needs or even broader social justice needs.[3] Responsive action can include direct care, preventing harm, listening and actively maintaining relationships, or helping to nurture children into becoming admirable moral teenagers and adults. A care perspective assumes and responds to dependence. As Virginia Held argues, care cannot be patronizing benevolence but rather it requires a quality and orientation that builds upon understanding and open engagement with others. Key questions to help think from an ethics of care perspective are summarized in textbox 4.6. Notice that care is about practices rather than a set of rules, and the practices of care require attentiveness, responsibility, and responsiveness to the concrete situation and unique individuals and social groups in which we are embedded.

TEXTBOX 4.6. CARE: KEY QUESTIONS

What needs are present in this context?

What does a caring response require in this setting?

Am I responding to the needs around me?

Whose voices am I hearing and not hearing?

Ubuntu. Ubuntu ethics similarly embrace the idea that we live interconnected and communal lives. The word Ubuntu comes from the Bantu languages found in east, central, and southern Africa. While translations are not exact, the meaning of the concept is frequently summed up in the phrase "a person is a person through other people." From this perspective, our lives are intertwined and bound together. We live and act based upon an empathic, relational worldview.

Retired Archbishop and former chairman of the South African Truth and Reconciliation Commission Desmond Tutu writes in *No Future without Forgiveness* that "a person with *Ubuntu* is open and available to others, affirming of others, does not feel threatened that others are able and good; for he or she has a proper self-assurance that comes with knowing that he or she belongs in a greater whole and is diminished when others are humiliated or diminished, when others are tortured or oppressed, or treated as if they were less than who they are" (1999, p. 31). Tutu notes that people with Ubuntu are generous and caring, compassionate and hospitable. What Ubuntu adds to our assessment of morality in peacebuilding is the consideration of the ways in which our work and our lives are intertwined with those with whom and for whom we are working and living, and thinking about how we might contribute to greater wholeness. Key questions to consider elements of Ubuntu ethics are presented in textbox 4.7. In the context of the Truth and Reconciliation Commission in South Africa, Ubuntu particularly helped to frame and support a restorative justice approach, which included efforts to reconcile and restore relationships between victims and offenders. This is an ethic that is often embedded in peacebuilding work.[4]

TEXTBOX 4.7. UBUNTU: KEY QUESTIONS

Do my actions contribute to our greater joint humanity?

Am I acting in a way that reflects and enriches our interdependence and solidarity?

When we consider Ubuntu and care, we think about what it means to be in moral relationships with others. We are committed to respect and respond to those communities as an integral part of the community. We can think about ourselves as moral actors that are not free agents but embedded within and responding to concentric circles of communities. These circles support and sustain us, and are ones to which we are responsible and for which we are responsible. Our challenge then is to contribute to these communities, even when we might think we are outsiders working within someone else's moral community in peacebuilding (e.g., a Nigerian working in Canada, or a Muslim working in a Christian community).

A central challenge for relationally oriented ethical thinking is how to deal with difference in a way that is just. In duty-based ethics, everyone has a duty to treat everyone else equally and the principle of equity is seen as creating the benchmark for what is just. In a relationally centered ethical system, there are times when the needs of particular people, or the relationship of those people to you, suggest a greater claim on you. For example, perhaps one group is more marginalized in a system and therefore needs more attention in order to help them become part of a post-conflict reconstruction effort. Or perhaps your organization is relationally more connected to a particular group. The challenge becomes one of responding to needs in a caring way that also reinforces the value of the larger community in which you are embedded and responds to not only material needs but also to larger social and political needs and concerns. Finally, a caring response will also need to include an element of self-care.

Care and Ubuntu together focus on the moral value of relationships and interdependence. Through care, we ask questions about what responsiveness requires in a giving setting, and how we can care for needs around us. Ubuntu provides us with a perspective of assessing our actions through their ability to contribute to the collective whole: Does our peacebuilding contribute to greater joint humanity? Do we enrich interdependence and solidarity through our peacebuilding work? These are important questions to include as we assess the ethics of practice.

Care and Ubuntu applied. In considering the question of whether or not we share our conflict analysis of Jos—which itself is a complex picture of grievances and issues that matter to those with whom we are in relationship—we need think about our positionality and relationality. We have been asked by security forces to share this information, and security forces represent some of the voices—often privileged voices—within our community. They are articulating some concerns to us in the request, such as their concern and responsibility for security in Jos. These are important considerations. Yet there are other voices in our community who fear these actors because they see them as siding with one or another side of the conflict, and one or another of the politicians' interests. From an ethic of care vantage point, we need to listen for and be responsive to the needs in Jos, as well as larger concentric circles of those with whom we are in relationship (e.g., thinking geographically this might be Plateau State, Nigeria, West Africa, and so forth). In listening, we hear calls for material needs to be met by those who are living on the margins of Jos, those who were displaced in earlier rounds of conflict, those who moved to Jos in hopes of finding jobs but who were not successful, those who are not able to go to school in Jos because they are not indigenes in the area, or those who have been displaced by violence in the north of Nigeria and Boko Haram's attacks. We hear complex calls to respond to physical, psychosocial, and vocational needs in Jos. We hear echoes of our conflict analysis in terms of whose voices feel excluded and marginalized in decisions and life in Jos and these, in many ways, reflect patterns of exclusion that persist more broadly in Nigeria.

Processing the request from an ethics of care and Ubuntu perspective involves placing the voices and issues within this larger community of concerns and responsiveness. We can ask: Does this request to share our conflict analysis information reinforce patterns of exclusion or reinforce the vulnerability of people with whom we are in relationship, and patterns which we are trying to address? Are these voices asking us to not simply share an analysis, but to do something more? In what ways can we contribute to working and living together well? If the answer to the question of exclusion is yes, it will reinforce patterns of exclusion and vulnerability, then we need to think about more caring ways to respond to the request that will enable parties to better hear and respond to needs (physical, psychological, social justice needs) in a caring way. This will be vitally important in order to answer yes to our Ubuntu questions, which are whether or not we are contributing to our collective humanity and whether or not we are enhancing our interdependence and solidarity through these actions. As evident from these questions, our first action is to listen and engage with those around us before deciding our course of action.

USING MORAL THEORIES IN PEACEBUILDING PRACTICE

Each of the moral theories presented above provide scaffolding to think through moral problems and challenges in our peace work: they focus on collective ends, responsibility (or duties) to persons, the character of ourselves as peacebuilders, as well as our relationality and interdependence. In table 4.1, the moral theories, foci, big ideas, and key questions are placed side by side. This table is intended to help peacebuilders ask key questions about our work as we inquire and deliberate on the moral values we will live out in the midst of our work. Not all of the questions or considerations will be equally relevant all of the time. But, when they are an integrated part of our usual patterns of thinking and practice, they can enhance our thinking to identify what is morally at stake in a particular decision or set of actions.

It may be helpful to think about the fit between moral questions and the phases of a project or program cycle. There typically are at least three phases: planning and design, implementation and monitoring, and project/program wrap-up and evaluation (with the final phase intended to inform the next program or project cycle).

Questions that capture different aspects of our moral values during the **design phase** of an initiative include: Whose voices are we listening to in designing our intervention? What does care and responsiveness require in this setting? What character traits are considered good and virtuous in this setting, and how do these ideas of what is virtuous relate to our work and approach to peacebuilding? Can we design a process that enables a regular check-in with

Table 4.1. Moral Theories Side by Side

Focus	*Moral Theory*	*Big Ideas*	*Key Questions*
Consequences	Consequentialism (Utilitarianism especially)	We must track intended and unintended consequences. Goodness depends on outcomes.	• What good will come from this action? (intended and unintended) • What harms will come from this action? (intended and unintended) • Will this action produce the best consequences overall?
Duties	Deontology or Duty-based ethics (can include rights and prima facie duties)	We must perform actions that are intrinsically good. Everyone has the same rights and responsibilities (universal obligations). Never treat people as a means to an end.	• What are the moral obligations and responsibilities that are required of everyone? Am I (are we) following our moral obligations? • Am I (are we) treating people as ends in and of themselves or as means to an end? • Are we treating everyone as having equal moral claims (rights)? • Are these moral obligations reasonable? (Would rational individuals consent?)
Virtues	Virtue Ethics	Focus on character and disposition. Pursuit of a life well-lived, which is constitutive of collective flourishing.	• What is considered virtuous in this context? Am I upholding these virtues? • Am I living a life well-lived? • What would a virtuous person do in this situation?
Relationships	Ethics of Care Ubuntu Ethics	Our lives are intertwined and we are interdependent. Responsiveness to needs around us is morally good. Whatever we do will contribute to (or detract from) our greater, collective whole.	• What needs are present in this context? • What does a caring response require in this setting? • Am I responding to the needs around me? • Whose voices am I hearing and not hearing? • Do my actions contribute to our greater joint humanity? • Am I acting in a way that reflects and enriches our interdependence and solidarity?

local peacebuilding moral exemplars as we proceed? What good effects and unintended negative effects might we expect from our planned intervention? How can we further the good effects and minimize the negative effects?

During **implementation** of our peacebuilding initiatives, we will ask questions that monitor our ethics in practice. For example, am I acting virtuously? Are we enacting moral values that contribute to flourishing in our activities? Are we treating people as ends or means to our end? Are we being responsive to others in our programming? Are we evidencing care? What intended positive effects are accruing? What negative effects are occurring, and how can we address them?

In the wrap-up and **evaluation** stage, it will be helpful to ask questions like: Did we do the right things? Did we maximize the good and minimize the harms? Did we contribute to our collective humanity and solidarity through this initiative? Which marginalized voices did we miss or ignore, and can we do something to respond to these voices now? If the answer to any of the first three questions is "no," then further exploration is required in order to shape more ethical initiatives in the future.

THREE CAUTIONS TO NOTE

There are some challenges and limits in using moral theories in our thinking. To avoid frustration and common pitfalls, it may be useful to think through what moral theories cannot provide, in addition to what they can provide. A first set of cautions relate to how we use moral theories to better our work. We want to avoid the hazards that come with moral theory in either using it like a weapon against others ("you were wrong and here's why!") or using moral theory to simply justify what we did or were thinking of doing anyway ("Of course my decision was right because it produced the best end!"). To avoid these hazards, keep thinking openly and carefully, as discussed in earlier chapters.

A second caution is to avoid paralysis and getting stuck. The point of using moral theories for applied ethics in peacebuilding is to help you develop your skills in open thinking that reflects upon peacebuilding from multiple moral value perspectives. If you find yourself running down one rabbit trail and following a particular line of logic so closely that it is paralyzing, then it's time to take a moment to pause and ask: "Are the questions that I am pursuing important—are they the questions I need to consider at this time?" What is morally important to attend to in this situation? It may be that the questions being asked are important, or it may be that while the questions are interesting they are not terribly relevant to the on-the-ground work at that moment.

A third caution to note is that working with multiple values means that, at times, they likely will come into conflict. In the Jos example explored above regarding sharing conflict analysis data, it appears that the greatest possible positive consequences are achieved if we allow some people to be harmed when the conflict analysis is shared with security forces and the broader public. This is in direct contrast to ethics of care and its demand for a response to needs as well as Kant's imperative to always treat people as ends and never as a means to an end. However, rather than viewing our values as an either/or dilemma, we can use the tension to expand our options of what is moral. Considering how to care for individuals with whom we are in relationship and a broader community, as well as how care is integral to happiness, can reframe our options. Our moral value concerns point to values that we want to respect in the process as well as the end product of our work. The tension between ends and means is helpful because we are forced to think more broadly and creatively than we might otherwise if thinking about only one moral value. The question of how to do this—how to turn a moral tension into a source for creativity—is the focus of chapter five.

In sum, moral theories can be useful as logical scaffolding to help draw attention to important values in the course of peacebuilding work. Recognizing the moral values foci as well as challenges associated with using moral theories is helpful to recognizing what is entailed in application and what is not addressed or provided within the logical scaffolding of the respective theories. Multiple moral theories help us get out of limited lines of thinking. Like the old adage that says everything looks like a nail if you have only a hammer, so too does everything look like an effect if you're only looking for consequences. Using questions generated by different moral theories can help us be more open and analytical thinkers who do not simply pick a favorite line of moral reasoning and use it to evaluate everything.

The moral values attended to in these five moral theories speak to significant considerations in peacebuilding today. They offer perspectives that can enlarge our understanding of what we think is good or right peacebuilding practice in order to help improve our ability to do good well. And, as Aristotle argued in *Nichomachean Ethics* (1103b 26–29), we investigate the nature of good not simply for the sake of knowing what good is but rather that we may become good.[5] We think about moral values and ethics in order to *be* ethical.

FOR FURTHER EXPLORATION

Here are some questions and activities that you can use to further think about issues raised in this chapter:

- To which moral theory are you most attracted? Why? Which moral theory do you find most challenging? Why?

- Imagine you are leading a peacebuilding team. Design an ethical reflection process that would use the moral theories. Be specific about when and how you would draw upon these moral theories in your ethical reflection process and how you would move toward a decision. (E.g., would everyone apply all of the moral theories? Would certain people apply certain theories? At what points in your reflection-action cycle do you use the moral theories to reflect?)
- Below are three peacebuilding scenarios. Use the moral theories to identify a holistic ethical response to the dilemma that is posed in one of the scenarios. Brainstorm a list of responses that would meet each of the moral theories. Once you've done that, work to think holistically and develop options that you think would be moral according to as many of the theories as you can.

Scenario 1: You are part of a team operating in a conflict-affected area where you need a translator. Your translator is a young, unmarried woman from an urban center, and your team is largely male and operating in a rural area where there are very strong religious prohibitions against young, unmarried women working with men (and staying in the same hotel as men). While your translator does not have a problem with this arrangement, you have begun to hear rumors about your translator's lack of honor, and your driver indicates he has heard two credible threats of attack against the entire team. You are in the middle of a participatory process that is gathering information for how to design a peacebuilding intervention in this area. Your translator has been a very good and reliable translator for your work and she sees this job as part of her own professional development and needs the money to support her aging parents. What are the moral issues that need to be considered here? How might you respond?

Scenario 2: You have worked on an inter-religious dialogue in your community with religious leaders from the main faith traditions for the past eight years. Over the years, you have established very good relations with the Islamic, Christian, Buddhist and Hindu leaders in your area. Peace Accords were signed two years ago, and since then you have been approached by many international aid organizations looking to financially support your work. You have thus far refused any support from international aid organizations because you did not want their foreign agendas to affect the quality and motives of your own organization's work. However, you are finding that you have fewer volunteers or sources of support now that the international community is engaging in peacebuilding projects in your area—it seems they have become competitors to your initiative. Another representative of a non-governmental organization funded by the European Union has asked to meet with you this week and is interested in working with you on an inter-religious peacebuilding project. What are the moral issues that need to be considered here? How might you respond?

Scenario 3: You are a new employee who has been asked to conduct a series of interviews with participants in a peacebuilding and livelihoods program in communities affected by violence. The areas to which you will travel are not easily accessible. You are going with a small team of local colleagues. The team members have all lived in the conflict zone and you have noticed that they sometimes react very strongly when rumors of violence ripple through the office. You think they may be affected by significant trauma. Last week, several bombings happened again in the area to which you will travel. You talk with the driver and discover that he is quite nervous about going, but has agreed to take the team because of the additional danger pay. Security reports from the government—which is what your organization relies upon for its risk assessments—indicate that the area is now secure. What are the moral issues that need to be considered before you go out to the community? How might you respond?

NOTES

1. For more detailed introductions to moral theories, which this chapter draws upon, see Mark Timmons's *Disputed Moral Issues* (second edition, New York: Oxford University Press, 2010), Section I ("A Moral Theory Primer"), Anthony Weston's *A 21st Century Ethical Toolbox* (third edition, New York: Oxford University Press, 2013), Section II ("Moral Values"), or Kimberly Hutching's review of moral theories as they relate to global ethics in *Global Ethics: An Introduction* (Malden, MA: Polity Press, 2010). The argument that James Sterba puts forward regarding the complementarity of moral theories is presented in his book *The Triumph of Practice over Theory in Ethics* (New York: Oxford University Press, 2005). Mary Anderson explores the injunction to "do no harm" in development work memorably in *Do No Harm: Supporting Capacities for Peace through Aid* (Boulder, CO: Lynne Rienner Publishers, Inc., 1996). For a contemporary exploration of the connection between human rights and moral theory, see Kimberly Hutchings (2010) Mark Timmons (2010), or an earlier exploration by J. L. Mackie in "Can There Be a Rights-Based Moral Theory?" (*Midwest Studies in Philosophy,* 3:350–59, 1978). It is in John Rawl's 1971 *A Theory of Justice* that the phrase "behind a veil of ignorance" is deployed (Cambridge, MA: Harvard University Press, p. 136).

2. Alasdair MacIntyre's *After Virtue: A Study in Moral Theory* (Notre Dame, IN: University of Notre Dame Press, 1981) provides a foundation for how to use

narratives in a contextualized modern virtue ethics; to see how a narrative approach to virtue ethics can be applied in peacebuilding, see Todd Whitmore's article "'If They Kill Us at Least the Others Will Have More Time to Get Away': The Ethics of Risk in Ethnographic Practice" (*Practical Matters*, 3:1–28, 2010). I work through how virtue ethics and multiple moral values apply in another peacebuilding scenario involving a police officer in East Timor in the article "Doing Good Better: Expanding the Ethics of Peacebuilding" (*International Peacekeeping*, 21(4):427–442, 2014).

3. Additional background on ethics of care is available in Carol Gilligan's *In a Different Voice: Psychological Theory and Women's Development* (Cambridge, MA: Harvard University Press, 1982), as well as in an updated overview by Virginia Held in "The Ethics of Care" in *The Oxford Handbook of Ethical Theory* (edited by David Copp; New York: Oxford University Press, 2006). H. Richard Niebuhr's relational ethics are explored in the posthumously published *The Responsible Self: An Essay in Christian Moral Philosophy* (New York: Harper & Row Publishers, 1963).

4. For more information on Ubuntu as a source for ethics, see Munyaradzi Felix Murove's edited volume *African Ethics: An Anthology of Comparative and Applied Ethics* (Scottsville, South Africa: University of KwaZulu-Natal Press, 2009), Desmond Tutu's *No Future without Forgiveness* (New York: Doubleday, 1999), or Ronald Nicolson's edited volume *Persons in Community: African Ethics in a Global Culture* (Scottsville, South Africa: University of KwaZulu-Natal Press, 2008). Tim Murithi explores the relationship between Ubuntu ethics and peacebuilding further in *The Ethics of Peacebuilding* (Edinburgh: Edinburgh University Press, 2009). For an exploration of the relationship between Ubuntu and Kantian ethics vis-à-vis international relations, see Mvuselelo Ngcoya's "Ubuntu: Toward an Emancipatory Cosmopolitanism?" (*International Political Sociology* 9 (3):248–62, 2015).

5. Aristotle's original quote in *Nichomacean Ethics* is "for we are not investigating the nature of virtue for the sake of knowing what it is, but in order that we may become good" (New York: Oxford University Press, 1103b, 26–29).

5

Creative Problem-Solving When Values Conflict

MORAL VALUE CONFLICTS

Often times, decisions about what is good and right are made with little difficulty. At other times, we find ourselves on the horns of a dilemma, painfully aware that either horn might harm us and others depending upon which horn we choose. Moral dilemmas present situations in which our choice is between only two options, either of which will violate a strongly held moral value (or moral imperative) if chosen. Moral dilemmas are the bread and butter of ethical debates. Dramatic dilemmas like "do you torture someone to get information" or "do you steal to save your dying child" present either–or choices where you must choose between values—such as saving many lives or violently harming one life in the first scenario, or saving one life and violating a moral rule from which everyone benefits in the second scenario.

Choosing between moral values that we hold dear presents us with a weighty conundrum. Many of us hold certain moral values as sacred (e.g., religious prohibitions against killing, lying); often these values help define us as they speak to who we are, our character, and our commitments. It is challenging to question where our values come from, the ways in which society has shaped our values, and which values are most important. In negotiation, it is clear that people get entrenched in particular positions because they see these positions as directly tied to their values (e.g., I refuse to negotiate because I am taking a stand against injustice in my community). The equating of a moral value with one position can block discussion and further entrench a conflict.

Generally, people do not look to negotiate values; as a colleague of mine once quipped, you can't conclude that "I will be unjust only on Tuesdays." Principled negotiation, made famous by Roger Fisher and William Ury's book *Getting to Yes*, focused on interests and needs and in doing so moved away both from firmly held positions as well as the danger of being mired in moral value debates. In the third edition of *Getting to Yes*, Fisher, Ury, and Patton note that "although people's religious convictions are unlikely to be changed through negotiation, the actions they take, even those based on their convictions, *may* be subject to influence" (2011, p. 166).[1] This final comment, that actions may be subject to influence, points to the space for seeing where and how we can think about creative problem-solving when values conflict.

Moral dilemma scenarios that allow for two and only two terrible choices are very rare; they are usually developed in order to test or refine moral arguments, and to develop them for an argument's sake requires considerable manipulation and imposing significant constraints on circumstances. For example, Michael Davis (2005) weighed the morality of the "ticking time bomb" scenario that is used to argue that torture is morally permissible in exceptional circumstances. In his analysis, he notes that the scenario requires circumstances that have never actually occurred although they have become a mainstay of television shows and films; it requires a fanatic bomber, a timed nuclear weapons device, *and* that this fanatic bomber be in custody during the crucial countdown time period. "Purified" of all contingencies, the scenario is presented as an either–or scenario: either torture the bomber or suffer the consequences of the bomb; even then, it rests upon a highly problematic assumption that torture produces reliable information.[2] The scenario, like many manufactured moral dilemmas, is a work of fiction that may crystalize a particular tension between values but bears very little resemblance to challenges encountered in everyday and exceptional security work.

One of the tremendous benefits of working in complex, unruly settings is that we are rarely, if ever, in situations where there are two and only two options in our peacebuilding work, nor do we live in places where there is only one way of living out a value that we hold dear. The sheer complexity of peacebuilding work is to our advantage in developing ethical responses. What constrains us is not a limited choice between two purified options, nor our values, but our own lack of creativity in generating ethical options. This is even the case when it seems as though we are confronting a moral dilemma, such as the example scenario involving corruption presented in textbox 5.1. A tension between competing values can signal an opportunity to open up space in order to think creatively and generate options.

The focus of this chapter is creative problem-solving. Creative problem-solving, non-dichotomous "both/and" thinking, and multi-partiality—representing all sides in a process—are at the heart of most conflict transformation and conflict resolution methodologies. This includes interest-based negotiation, interactive problem-solving workshops, mediation, other alternative

TEXTBOX 5.1. MOVING BEYOND A FALSE DICHOTOMY: A WEST AFRICAN EXAMPLE

A NGO was in the process of setting up a new peacebuilding project in a country in West Africa. As part of project set-up, the project manager visited various community leaders including the elected political official in the area in order to inform him of what was going on and to show respect as well as build a relationship. The project involved setting up an early warning system throughout a strategic area that was violence-prone during elections. An effective early warning system required liaising with security personnel and government officials for follow-up if there were reported incidents that might flare up into greater violence. At the meeting, the politician asked for money to support the early warning initiative. The project management staff was taken aback as this was not in the plan. The organization had strict funding and accountability guides, a head office in North America, and this appeared to be a clear request for a bribe or a kickback.

Staff members could have reacted to the presenting situation as a narrow dilemma: I am implicated in corruption or I take a stand against it. They could have also reacted in a way that would have insulted the politician and shut down relationships with government at least for a time. Instead, NGO staff members thought about the moral values at stake in the interaction and developed a creative alternative.

First, they recognized there were multiple moral values at play—the right thing to do was understood in different ways in the situation by various groups involved in the process. There were the NGO's values of not supporting corruption and pursuing transparency, there were also the values the politician and larger community held, which involved social norms around recognizing others and being respectful members of society. The NGO team expanded the project to include the politician in the early warning system itself. In doing so, they provided him with the same type of phone that all of the other participants in the early warning network received. This enabled the politician to be properly respected and recognized, which was an important value to him, and the organization to enact its value of transparency and accountability. It also meant that the government itself would be part of the process of preventing election-related violence. The moral value tension disappeared with creative, additive thinking.

dispute resolution mechanisms, scenario thinking, as well as a wide range of bridge-building, relational, and structural transformation activities that go into peacebuilding. Working to expand options rather than viewing situations as zero-sum gains is an important part of the field.

Anthony Weston, an American ethicist, has adapted conflict resolution methodologies to enhance ethical deliberation in his book *Creative Problem-Solving in Ethics* (2005). This chapter builds on his work and utilizes creative problem-solving for ethics in conflict resolution and peacebuilding contexts and applications. In what follows, I discuss creative problem-solving generally and five heuristic devices specifically that can help generate creative thinking. This is followed by a discussion of how to make decisions after options have been generated. Finally, the chapter explores what creative problem-solving can look like concretely in peacebuilding initiatives in Afghanistan and western Canada.

CREATIVE PROBLEM-SOLVING

To get off of what appears to be the horns of a dilemma, we need a bit of mental space to rethink our situation and to reimagine what it is we are trying to accomplish. We can use the discomfort that value tensions generate in order to propel us to reflect and respond in better ways. When confronting a dilemma, our first task is to find out as much as we can about the problem. Finding out as many details as possible provides a more complete picture of what is going on, and a stronger base for moral decision-making. Understanding the context better provides an opportunity for re-thinking the problem. It also sets the stage for creative problem-solving.

Knowing more about the facts of the situation is complemented by expanding knowledge of the values at stake. Identifying moral values (the focus of chapter 3) is a critical part of ethical reflection-action. In situations where you believe there is a value conflict or dilemma, it becomes particularly important to understand what is at stake for actors in a particular decision or line of action. In the case in textbox 5.1, knowing the details about social norms and expectations around respect were important in order to understand which moral values were priorities and informed thinking about alternatives for how they could be met. If one has deep contextual knowledge, identifying these values can occur through private reflections. If, however, one is working in another moral community, where people may hold different assumptions about what is right and good, then sharing our concerns and understanding with others and listening to other's responses will be especially important. Colleagues, local gatekeepers, and trusted advisors—some of the moral value stakeholders pictured in figure 3.1—can help discern the full range of moral values that are implicated and appear to be in conflict.

At times, some moral values may have negative or harmful dimensions to them, or rather to the behavior that is routinely enacted based upon the moral value. Honor killings and revenge, for example, fall into this category of actions taken based upon particular understandings of moral codes of behavior. How can peacebuilders engage with these kinds of values in peace work? The case example presented in textbox 5.2 provides insight into how to respond. In this case, the value of revenge needed to be examined as it was confounding all attempts at mediation. In the end, the mediator used the tension as a point of departure for a discussion, which enabled the group to move beyond a persistent roadblock.

After generating a full list of values at stake, prioritize which values are most important for the different stakeholders and then generate options for how to respond. It is here that creative problem-solving is particularly needed in order to expand options for what we can actually do about the problem. The question becomes: How do we engage in ways that allow us to meet multiple values that on the surface appear to conflict? Reframing the situation as an opportunity enables us to generate new insights, options, and choices. Using heuristic devices, such as brainstorming, can be useful in this process because they encourage generating unexpected and inventive new lines of thinking.[3]

TEXTBOX 5.2. CONTENDING VALUES IN MEDIATION

A well-seasoned South African mediator working in a neighboring country was confounded by the value that was placed on revenge by the groups with whom he was mediating. Perplexed, he eventually chose to share his dilemma with someone whom he could trust would not violate his confidentiality (note that the value of moving forward in the mediation is prioritized here over absolute secrecy, although the confidentiality of participants was fully maintained). The listener asked, "What do you do when revenge comes up?" And the mediator replied, "I've just been avoiding it." The listener then shared a story of how they used to deal with problems in community disputes: "When we didn't know what to do, we put it on the agenda." Putting revenge on the mediator's agenda for the parties allowed the parties to air their concerns and eventually reframed the discussion from revenge to justice. Reframed, they got into a discussion of what really mattered to the parties, which transformed the mediation process.

Five heuristic devices are offered below to aid the process: brainstorm, wild associations, utopian thinking, healthy contradictions, and case comparisons.

Brainstorm. Great brainstorm sessions are like fierce rain storms where ideas fall fast and furious upon receptive soil. Here there are no filters to inhibit the ideas that tumble out of our mouths and into collective awareness. Some brainstorm experts suggest developing two hundred to four hundred ideas in the first five minutes! We may not all be able to get to this number, but it is helpful to think about because it sets an ambitious goal which we can keep in mind in order to push ourselves to develop more options. Often ideas generated later in brainstorming are more creative than the early ideas. If we stop too soon, we undercut the process.

The point of brainstorming is to contribute new ideas or build off of others' ideas positively. Brainstorming sessions are constrained when people rule out ideas as soon as they are proposed. People may respond to ideas prematurely with comments that shut down idea generation by saying things like: "that will never work," or "I like it, but. . . ." Notice that "but," while a little word, immediately signals a close to a particular line of thinking. When brainstorming, work at curbing tendencies to undermine or over-value other people's ideas, and focus on additive thinking. Typically, this requires the group to enforce a "no discussion, no evaluation" rule, which can take practice. Reframe the "but" that a colleague voices into an "and" statement in a way that helps add to the list. Textbox 5.3 offers a few more ideas to support productive brainstorming sessions. Brainstorming is often a great way for groups to expand their creative thinking because it enables them to accumulate as many options as possible within a pre-set period of time.

Create wild associations. Using wild or random associations is another way to spark creative thinking, which can be used within a group brain-

TEXTBOX 5.3. TIPS FOR BRAINSTORMING

- Strictly enforce the "no discussion, no evaluation" rule.
- Record responses that seem to repeat previous responses as they can capture distinctive aspects of the issue for different people.
- Keep going—innovation tends to start after the first fifty ideas.
- Use two people to record.
- Stimulate lateral thinking by using wild associations.

storming session or on its own. The idea is to use random images, words, or analogies, to work off of and develop new ideas. Look around and pick two different objects at random (e.g., a coffee cup and a maple tree were in my visual range when I first wrote this), and then use these objects as the starting point for new, lateral thinking. The objects will often conjure up images or provide analogies to use in devising new ways to respond to a problem. An example of how to begin using wild associations to brainstorm responses on a problem like corruption is presented in textbox 5.4. The idea behind choosing random objects or words is that it pushes us to freely associate and expand our creative potential.

Describe utopias. Another technique to enhance creative thinking is to dream up ideal solutions, and then slowly work your way toward what might work in the current context. Develop an image of what you want to see—a

TEXTBOX 5.4. WILD ASSOCIATIONS: A COFFEE CUP . . . AND CORRUPTION?

A coffee cup or a maple tree . . . how can one of these objects help us think creatively about the value conflict presented in textbox 5.1? Here are some examples of how thinking about a coffee cup, or maple tree, just might be a springboard for new ideas:

- A coffee cup can hold coffee as well as other liquids. If our relationship is the coffee cup, what else might it contain?
- A coffee cup is used for containing hot liquids that might burn us. Can we think of containing the negative aspects of a request for a bribe in the same way? What is the container we need to construct? What is the good that we want to get out?
- Some coffee cups have wide mouths and others have narrow mouths. Can we think of the shape of our approach as helping to achieve the good we want to get out? Is the mouth of our approach too wide? Too narrow? Are we causing drips?
- Maple trees produce sap, and sugar maple trees produce so much sap that we can make maple syrup. Boiling maple sap into syrup takes a long time; it takes something like forty liters of sap to make one liter of syrup. Have we tried to move too quickly? Is our sap (our perceived value of transparency) not yet syrup? What else do we need to do?
- Add your ideas here.

utopia. Then, slowly work your way into understanding different ways to achieve this utopia, or identifying what of this utopian vision is most achievable. As Elise Boulding and John Paul Lederach, among others, have pointed out, peacebuilding work is often inspired by visionary thinkers who are able to see what a just peace looks like beyond their current, violence-plagued, and unjust lived experiences.[4] We can use visionary thinking and our moral imaginations for envisioning peace and responding to the ethical challenges and dilemmas that arise along the way.

Healthy contradictions. While brainstorming deliberately avoids negative feedback, a healthy contradictions approach purposively utilizes opposing perspectives as a source for new ideas through structured debate. Purposefully ask people to put forward arguments that represent opposing positions. Ask people to represent a position that is not their own for the exercise; this step is important to help ensure people do not get further tied to their opinions as can happen during debates. Ask each person, or a team, to develop a line of argumentation based upon a given perspective or position. Once people have developed their line of argumentation, engage in a time-bound debate about what is right and good, and why it is right and good. Follow this session with an integrative thinking session where people offer ideas to bridge the different values and respond as ethically as possible. You might also include a "listening team" as a third side during the structured debate whose responsibility it is to get the integrative thinking going by identifying significant values and points of concerns for both sides (see textbox 5.5).

An approach that uses contrasting viewpoints in a structured way can be helpful to ward off any tendency for a group to engage in groupthink. Groupthink refers to the faulty decision-making process psychologist Irving Janis observed in groups that come to consensus too quickly in order to preserve group collegiality; if unity is prioritized over full discussion in a decision-making process, groups ignore important information, and produce suboptimal and even problematic decisions, which is explored further in chapter 6.[5]

Case comparisons. Sometimes it is helpful to compare and contrast the case you are looking at with another case in order to help people think about different aspects or dimensions of the original case. The case you compare your situation to may be similar to the one you are confronting, and in other ways quite unique. When comparing your situation to another in order to help you respond to a moral dilemma, look for what was done in the situation, why it was done, and the outcomes it achieved. Then compare and contrast the choices and context to your own case. You might purposefully choose positive cases for comparison; positive cases here refer to cases where you feel people made very ethical choices and you are looking to make similar types of choices. For example, you compare your situation to that of a colleague

TEXTBOX 5.5. A HEALTHY CONTRADICTIONS EXERCISE USING MORAL THEORIES

The healthy contradictions approach can be modified to draw out different moral theory perspectives and foci. The following format can be used with groups of four or five, or larger groups if people are divided into moral theory teams.

Step 1: Formulate an argument
Assign a unique moral theory perspective to each member of a group of four or five (if working with a group of ten, assign to each pair a moral theory perspective). Use the moral theories summarized in chapter 4 to help guide each person's thinking, or draw upon other moral perspectives that are deemed important for the context. Allocate ten minutes for each individual or team to brainstorm a response to an ethical tension in peacebuilding, applying their assigned moral theory perspective. Make sure that each person (or team) is applying the moral theory they were asked to apply, and not defaulting to another preferred way of thinking as your aim is to produce divergent lines of moral thinking. Ask people to develop an argument that does not fully represent their own opinion of what an ethical response entails, which might mean assigning them a moral theory perspective with which they do not resonate.

Step 2: Structure debate
Have each person (or team) report out and share his or her proposed response(s) to the ethical dilemma based upon the assigned moral theory perspective. Then open up the debate and ask people to argue for or against particular aspects of the responses (they can even argue against their own proposed response). Encourage healthy debate for a limited period of time (e.g., thirty minutes). It will be useful to generate a list of values that people are naming and upon which they disagree during the debate.

Step 3: Integrative thinking
After the debate, spend another thirty minutes identifying points of consensus and integrative options for responding to the moral value dilemma. You might find it helpful to have a "listening team" whose members are not directly debating, but whose responsibility it is to track the values that are named in the debate and identify potential points for integration.

Step 4: Choose from the options (see "Choosing Between Options") whom you uphold as an ethical exemplar, when he or she made a tough but good decision in responding to a similar problem.

Alternatively, you might choose negative cases for comparison; these are cases where you feel people made very poor ethical decisions and you are looking to avoid making similarly poor decisions. For example, many development organizations used their work in Rwanda prior to 1994 as an instance of moral failing that illustrated their own lack of attentiveness to social divisions and deep-rooted conflict. Development work prior to the 1994 genocide in Rwanda in general failed to be sensitive to or to address the deep rooted conflict and social divisions that existed, and in many cases reinforced and even amplified the divisions by the way development programming was conducted.[6] Development organizations used their experiences in Rwanda for internal learning about what went wrong, and have compared other development initiatives in divided societies to those that occurred in Rwanda prior to the genocide to more carefully engage in conflict-sensitive analysis and programming. An example of a conflict resolution technique that uses case comparisons is interactive problem-solving workshops, which are described in textbox 5.6. Here case comparisons can include exposure trips to other conflict contexts in order to shift deeply entrenched thinking.[7]

Brainstorming, wild associations, using utopias, healthy contradictions, and case comparisons are five heuristics to support creative problem-solving. There are many other creative techniques to consider that can promote expansive thinking, such as role playing, changing the scale of the problem that you are looking at (e.g., moving from focusing on a community-wide conflict to analyzing the conflict as it might affect a family, or vice versa), or trying to prove your greatest supporter (or critic) wrong. The unifying theme in all of them is that they are intended to help us reimagine and rethink the problems we are facing, including moral value tensions.

CHOOSING BETWEEN OPTIONS

The creative thinking stage generates many options. The next step is to choose between options. It is here, at this stage, that we become more critical of our ideas, and the advantages and disadvantages of different options. Our challenge at this point is to decide a course of action based upon the options before us.

An initial screen to use to facilitate making the best decision is to identify the option that meets multiple, prioritized moral values simultaneously. It might be the case that one response stands out as meeting multiple values and really seems to be the best. If we are working in a team, we can then move

TEXTBOX 5.6. PROBLEM-SOLVING WORKSHOPS AND CASE COMPARISONS

Interactive problem-solving workshops are a conflict resolution technique that bring together a relatively small group of mid-level, influential people from different sides of a deeply rooted conflict to build relationships among those involved in the workshops, and engage in collective problem-solving. One of the ways that problem-solving workshop facilitators like Herbert Kelman (professor emeritus from Harvard University) look to get people from deeply entrenched conflicts to think in new ways is to explore other cases. Kelman's problem-solving workshops, which primarily occurred between the 1970s and the 1990s, centered on participants from Israel and Palestine. Together participants explored their own conflict and perspectives, as well as used cases to expand their thinking. Kelman's group sometimes had outsiders join the workshops to present another case as a heuristic device. Kelman also brought problem-solving workshop participations to other conflict settings, such as Cyprus and Northern Ireland. These visits provided opportunities for Israeli and Palestinian participants to expand their thinking about their own conflict setting by focusing on another context, its dynamics, peace initiatives, challenges, and opportunities. While each setting and conflict was unique, there were points for comparison and contrast, which unlocked new ways of thinking about their own situation and possible ways forward. Kelman's group discovered they were able to generate creative options even for the most troubled and difficult elements of the Israeli–Palestinian conflict.

forward quickly with a consensus or strong majority decision (providing we have already taken steps to avoid groupthink). It may also be that while one response is generally better, it can be modified further to build agreement in areas where there seem to be differences of opinion. In both of these cases, decisions are relatively easy and straightforward.

On some occasions, the options may appear to be roughly equivalent. We may also find not all of the values are met equally in the options we are contemplating and we feel we are deciding between which moral values we prioritize. In situations like this, how do we decide between the options? Various ways to approach this challenge are listed below. Note that considerations of power dynamics and the question of "whose values count" in the decision-making process will need to be attended to in the process of decision-making to ensure it models and follows moral values. If we are making a personal decision, it is important that we can make decisions about our own actions and engagement and not feel like we are overlooking our own values. If we are working in a team, then there is a larger collective of people involved in the decision and a collective process of engagement is required. Further, if we are making decisions that affect other people's lives, we will ask: How will we engage those who will be affected by this decision? What say do people have about decisions that affect their lives?

Options to consider in order to facilitate ethical decision-making are:

- **Select a decision-making procedure in advance.** If everyone agrees on how the decision-making procedure will proceed, and agrees that the decision-making procedure itself is fair, then people will be more satisfied with the decision, even if some of the outcomes are ones with which they disagree. For example, common procedures for a team or partnership are to decide ethical choices through consensus, or through a 70 percent majority vote. Alternatively, you might appoint an ethical team leader who will make choices for the team based upon some pre-established criteria (e.g., the decision that meets the most values possible). An established procedure enables people to know what is happening in advance and can assist a group in coming to a quick decision.
- **Prioritize.** Think about whether or not we can prioritize values and what matters most in the specific decision context in which we are working. If so, then prioritize a response in a way that is both workable and fair to multiple stakeholders, giving particular consideration to those who are the most vulnerable.
- **Sequence.** Consider what might happen if nothing is done. Is this a problem? Is there an order in which actions might helpfully unfold? If it is important to do something and sequencing is helpful, design a response and follow it in a transparent way so stakeholders are fully aware of why the sequencing decision was taken, as well as how and when their values will be attended. Consider in what ways sequencing decisions are fair, just, responsive, and contribute to flourishing.
- **Consult.** Consult with others to determine what matters most, such as others in our profession, key local advisors, and moral exemplars as suggested in chapter 3. Consult professional ethical standards if they are available. There are some examples of principles in the field of peacebuilding that we can consult to help us think about value divergence (see recommendation in the Notes section).[8]
- **Mitigate risks and harms.** Think about the probabilities of risk and harms. Are there some risks that are greater and have more negative

consequences if they occur, which we need to prioritize mitigating? If so, then do this first. Or, are there ways to limit or reconfigure a negative outcome from a particular decision? This is particularly important to consider if it is clear that there will be some negatives regardless of which course of action we take, even after doing our best creative thinking.

- **Be responsive.** Use difficult decisions as opportunities to build relationships and understanding, where we look for and build upon areas of common agreement. This helps us to reorient towards responsiveness and an ethic of care in the process of our decision-making. There may be ways to use decision-making as ways of building bridges.
- **Agree to disagree.** We may find that sometimes we need to agree to disagree, and that we can still continue to collaborate in areas where our values are similar. We may discover that we do not share every value with other peacebuilders, and yet we can find values that we hold in common or are complementary and thus become the focus of our decision.

The above strategies can assist when making a difficult decision that involves moral values that are in conflict. The process used to decide will necessarily be informed by the context, and include considerations of culture and power, which were explored in chapters 2 and 3. They are methods that can be used within peacebuilding teams and organizations, as well as communities. After thinking creatively and making a decision, we then need to act carefully, deliberately, and decisively. We also need to be alert to when things may not go as planned and revise our course of action.

There are times that creative thinking will be messier than these neat heuristics suggest. Below are two examples of situations in which people have worked to address moral value tensions creatively in peacebuilding practice. The first example focuses on Afghanistan and involves actors navigating the dilemma between slow participatory processes and quick-impact alternatives in peacebuilding after war. Two program initiatives from Afghanistan are contrasted, which operate on overlapping and divergent moral values. One focuses primarily on positive consequences understood as the immediate provision of resources to bolster security and political order, and the other focuses on process considerations, relationality, and respect as well as providing resources to communities to respond to need and bolster political order. The contrast helps highlight the ways in which the second approach intentionally and creatively built on multiple values that appeared to be in tension, and was very well received within Afghanistan. The second case example explored below is from Canada. It provides an illustration of the ways in which additional research into a problem and changing moral value priorities (in part a result of utopian thinking) have altered responses to a land-related conflict in a western Canadian farming community. Together, the examples from Afghanistan and Canada provide us with ideas for how people have considered and addressed multiple moral values simultaneously, even in difficult circumstances.

CREATIVE PROBLEM-SOLVING I: QUICK IMPACTS VERSUS SLOW ENGAGEMENT IN AFGHANISTAN

A much-discussed dilemma in peacebuilding literature involves a trade-off between short-term and long-term peacebuilding (for further reading see the Notes section).[9] The former involves compromised approaches to peacebuilding which provide quick "peace dividends" that are understood to contribute to stability, but often require collaboration with warlords, entrenched elites, or former combatant leaders in ways that reinforce long-standing divisions within the conflict context. The long-term participatory approach to peacebuilding involves community members broadly and is intended to build local relationships and decision-making capacity, but takes more time to develop and may not address immediate issues of insecurity that can spiral into larger instability. In both of these scenarios, external actors are understood to play a supporting role, although external actors engage in direct implementation in the first model of quick peace dividends and necessarily play a facilitating role in the second approach.

At stake in this dilemma are several competing values about what constitutes good ends and the right way to do peacebuilding work. Considerations of what constitutes good ends variably include: security, stability, responding to community needs, local ownership, a fair and just society (sometimes framed as participatory democracy), and a caring society that enacts its values and collectively flourishes. Understandings of right means here include a duty to protect civilians and the principle of participatory engagement and local leadership. Typically, the values of security, stability, and to a lesser degree a duty to protect (on which quick impacts are based) are seen as being at odds with participatory engagement, local ownership, and caring for communities (on which longer-term participatory peacebuilding is based). In moral theory terms, duties and consequences are set against relationality, and to a lesser degree virtues.

The international peacebuilding that sets the backdrop for this exploration of a creative response to moral value tensions begins after the 2001 Bonn Agreement, negotiated by the international and national coalition after defeating the Taliban. Peacebuilding in Afghanistan at this time was directly tied to statebuilding in the context of a transitional government, insecurity, several decades of conflict, and a complex array of strongly self-reliant and independent groups in Afghanistan. Afghanistan's unique history and geography added further intricate layers. One of the significant questions that confronted decision-makers, then, was how to establish legitimate political authority and security in this context.[10]

Quick Impact Projects (QIP) were designed as one part of a response. This type of programming largely operated on the set of moral values noted above regarding quick response projects, including the moral values of order, stability, security, and protecting lives, underpinned by a consequentialist moral value perspective emphasizing the speed of achieving certain ends. A number of international donors provided substantial funds for relatively small, short-term projects in communities to help "win hearts and minds" in order to ensure stability in Afghanistan, and to decrease support for the Taliban—aid was defined as a nonlethal weapon to facilitate defeating an insurgency. Projects included building roads and water systems, as well as constructing or rehabilitating public and government buildings. For example, in 2003, USAID in Afghanistan established the Provincial Reconstruction Team Quick Impact Project (PRT-QIP), and the U.S. Department of Defense similarly launched a Commanders Emergency Response Program (CERP). CERP alone received approximately 3.4 billion U.S. dollars between 2004 and 2012 (Tarnoff, 2012, p. 20). QIP projects were to be implemented in coordination with government officials in order to connect and increase the confidence between communities and district, provincial, and central government bodies. It sought to achieve the greatest effect in terms of providing speedy "peace dividends" for communities and was intended to shore-up support for government, develop cooperative relations with the military, produce stability, and demonstrate the possibility of future political and economic progress.

There were, however, numerous problems. In general, quick assistance projects have been viewed very negatively in Afghanistan and suspected of contributing to corrupt practices and elite's pocketing resources (resources listed in the Notes section). More QIP funds were designated for highly conflictual areas than areas with less conflict, which had an unintended negative effect of appearing to reward communities that experienced greater overt conflict. The emphasis on speed and security meant that QIP projects were assessed as good based on the amount of money spent, projects completed, and people reached. While QIP projects were supposed to include a technical assessment and involve communities and government officials, these aspects were viewed as a means to an end of generating security, and therefore were of limited scope and duration. QIP projects were viewed as generating "'consent' (and therefore force protection) and facilitating 'conflict termination'" by PRTs rather than responding to other values and priorities (Bennet et al., 2009, p. 30). Military officers were encouraged to do more projects in less time to show results, which often did not respond to broad-based needs nor build local capacity. In some places, the peace dividends themselves contributed to local conflict in terms of groups vying for resources, or becoming targets of attack. The narrow focus further meant that other important sources of conflict, such as "corrupt and predatory activities" of local officials and police, were not addressed, which has further alienated people (Fishstein and Wilder, 2012, p. 29). Overall, the emphasis on understanding peace dividends as a means to short-term stability as an end (understood as military security) meant that other important moral values that constitute what is good and right were overlooked and even undermined, which unfortunately produced significant negative consequences.

The National Solidarity Program (NSP), in contrast, is a program that is widely seen as successful in Afghanistan. It provides an example of how, under the same pressures, a large-scale effort was undertaken to creatively meet the multiple values of participation, community engagement, trust- and relationship-building, participatory decision-making as well as contributing to order, stability, and the promotion of a more participatory form of democracy. While I am framing this as a positive example of meeting multiple needs creatively, I should note that it is not without critiques and limitations, such as the important question of whether or not these moral values represent moral communities in Afghanistan (see Monsutti's article listed in the Notes section as well as the evaluations of NSP for greater detail).

The idea for the NSP itself came from a case comparison. Then finance minister of Afghanistan, Ashraf Ghani (now president), approached a former World Bank colleague to consider the applicability for Afghanistan of a previous, highly successful, large, Indonesian community development initiative from the 1990s. Ghani invited Scott Guggenheim, his former colleague, to Kabul to develop an Afghan version of the initiative, building upon the previous project but tailored to Afghanistan's context and values. Interesting for our purposes of creative problem-solving, Guggenheim (2004) reports that the initial project idea in Indonesia itself was developed to meet multiple values simultaneously: to address poverty, respond to and support local development initiatives, avoid money being syphoned off by local leaders and interlocutors, and build on past successful models of community development in Indonesia.

NSP is known as the flagship program of the government of Afghanistan. It is run by the Ministry of Rural Rehabilitation and Development and prioritizes community-driven development. It began in 2003 as an ambitious effort to support wide-scale participatory processes to identify and respond to community needs through the careful formation of elected Community Development Councils (CDCs). Facilitating partners utilize participatory rural appraisal processes to establish inclusive CDCs. Every adult in the community (male and female) have an equal vote, and further, the composition of the CDC is intended to be 50 percent male and 50 percent female. Once elected, CDCs meet to identify community needs, select projects for the community, and then develop proposals that are submitted to the ministry for potential funding. The ministry then provides block grants of up to $60,000 to communities, based on an allocation of $200 per household in the community. Communities are also required to contribute resources to the projects they propose. Following ministry approval of projects, the CDC is involved in the implementation, and ensures accountability for the allocation of resources.

The NSP design supports a number of moral values that might otherwise be seen as being in tension. NSP retains elements of consequentialism in that it is also pursuing the greatest effects through reaching as many communities as possible across Afghanistan—as of 2013, some 32,000 CDCs had been formed in 361 districts, which include locations in all thirty-four provinces in Afghanistan (Beath et al., 2015, p. viii). However, the other moral values that are foregrounded are community respect, responsiveness to community-defined needs (including reduced poverty), collaborative decision-making, trust and trust-building, relationships, inclusivity, transparency, self-reliance, and accountability. It does this through the implementing structure of community development councils and the granting mechanism. Interestingly, the good of enhanced security and stability also appears to be connected to CDCs, although this is less clearly a byproduct and there are conflicting assessments in this regard. Inger Boesen notes that the CDC structure builds upon a common, locally held moral good of community cooperation for the improvement of community in Afghanistan, known as *ashar* (2004, pp. 27–28). Further, the requirement of a community contribution also reinforces traditional norms of self-reliance and independence from foreign aid.

The CDC in each community operates as the linchpin in the NSP community development design. The process of creating community councils has involved very careful facilitation and trust-building by a group called facilitating partners—this trust-building and community mobilization process takes considerable time. The facilitating partners, which often include local persons on their staff, shepherd the creation of the CDC and support it in its process of developing proposals for the Ministry. Partner organizations use participatory rural appraisal techniques, which are highly interactive to identify community needs, map stakeholders, and reduce the degree to which decisions are dominated by elite or warlord concerns and priorities.

One area where the NSP has encountered resistance is with respect to involving women. This includes voting to elect community development council members, as well as female CDC members meeting with and making decisions with men regarding which projects to select to develop into full proposals for the Ministry. As Boesen observes, the NSP structure suggests very different norms than those of *purdah,* which are present in many rural areas of Afghanistan. In these areas, a family and a woman's honor is protected when women are in the private sphere, and participation in public is considered shameful. Partner organizations and communities have addressed this value tension in a variety of ways, which also evidence creative problem-solving. Communities are identified geographically and often can be considered more "private" because families tend to live near each other. In some communities, CDC elections occurred with women voting inside a person's home in order to preserve privacy. Frequently, a separate women's *shura* or committee is elected to develop ideas which are shared with the men's committee. In some cases, CDCs have proceeded in decision-making without women. In other cases, women and men's groups meet simultaneously but with a barrier between them. To address the challenge that only men's projects were being prioritized by CDCs, in some communities a certain percentage of funds were set aside for the women's committee projects. Finally, some CDCs have functioned with men and women participating, and in one community a woman was elected as the leader of the CDC. The flexibility of the program and the slow and careful nature of participatory rural appraisal techniques have allowed creative options to be generated in order to secure resources, address a value with respect to women's participation as well as respect cultural norms regarding honor, and to foreground participation and responsiveness.

In sum, the NSP provides a large-scale example of an initiative that valued the participatory process as a good, it also embodied respect for communities, local moral values of communities (e.g., honor and community cooperation), transparency in the process of elections and decision-making, as well as local accountability for fund allocations. The initiatives also needed to produce ends to meet the community defined needs to solidify the sense that something really was changing. The facilitating partner organizations sought to uphold multiple values at the same time ensuring that the understanding of good was not dominated by consequences, but also involved ethics of care and relationality, and particular duties for people country-wide and not just in highly conflict-affected communities. Evaluations of the NSP overall indicate that perceptions of the process as well as completed projects have been very positive although there are also numerous lessons and learnings as the program evaluations indicate (see the Notes section). In comparison with the quick impacts projects program design, it illustrates an adaptive and creative response to simultaneously pursue the moral value goods of stability understood in terms of community engagement, responsiveness, and participation, and in so doing combined consequentialism, duty-based imperatives, and relational moral values.

The second example of creative problem-solving in practice focuses on a case in which there has been a slow but clear reordering of moral values in the process of building peace in western Canada. Unlike the example from Afghanistan, it has evolved over time with no international attention, and it has not been formulated in terms of a project or program with outputs and timelines (which itself is instructive). Creative thinking and rethinking about moral values that are in tension occurred largely because of research and information gathering and, to a lesser degree, utopian thinking.

CREATIVE PROBLEM-SOLVING II: RETHINKING MORAL VALUES AROUND STONEY KNOLL IN CANADA

This case centers on a land-related indigenous-settler conflict, and peacebuilding efforts to respond to this conflict. The conflict emerged in overt form in 1976, when a small group of men claiming to represent the Young Chippewayan (an indigenous, First Nations band) unexpectedly visited and confronted farmers in the area of Stoney Knoll (Pwashemow Chakatanow in Cree), which is located in the Canadian province of Saskatchewan. Farmers were told by the visitors to take care of the land, as it was to be returned to the Young Chippewayan, to which at least one farmer reportedly retorted, "over my dead body." Divergent views of land and land ownership frequently occur as part of deep-rooted conflicts. The very idea of a right to own property is contested in many places as a dimension of indigenous-settler conflicts, as is the question of who and what types of rights to land individuals or groups of people might have (e.g., access to and use of land and land-based resources on the surface area, minerals and water below the surface, as well as the space above).[11]

The initial resistance and angry response of the farmers, as well as the confrontational words of the carload of young men, reflected strong moral claims in demanding justice and a recognition of rights and legitimacy. Each group felt very strongly that they were in the right in their claim to the land. The farmers held legal title to the land, which had been acquired properly per the property laws in Canada after the 1882 Dominion Lands Act. The Young Chippewayan claim was based on Treaty Six, also a legal document that the Government of Canada had written, signed, and was obliged to recognize, although mediated through a court claims process. From a legal perspective undergirded by a duty-based view of rights and obligations within a social contract, their claims were both right.

Initially, the conflict produced a stand-off of sorts, with fears of future confrontation. A church-affiliated non-governmental organization connected to the community heard about the dispute and, a year later, hired a consultant to research the history of Mennonite block settlements in the area; the researcher also added specific content on the Young Chippewayan land claim out of his own interest. This church-related group was motivated by their moral values around care and being responsive to the needs of those around as well as restoring relationships as part of a vision of restorative justice that was framed and undergirded by their faith. The efforts of this church-related group, however, generated very strong pushback from a sizable group of farmers in the area a year later. The farmers argued that the church-based organization should not be involved in the issue as it pertained to their livelihood; they argued that the matters were best left for the courts to decide—they valued the legal process itself as a guarantor of fairness and justice with an overall expectation that the courts would ensure the greatest good for the greatest number in Canada.

The research into the claim proved to be very important in helping people think about the moral values at stake. The carload of young men in 1976 had startled the farmers and awakened the community to a conflict of which they were ignorant. Research indicated that the farms were indeed part of an area that was set aside as a Reserve for the Young Chippewayan (also spelled Chipeewayan) as part of the provisions identified in Treaty Six. This treaty, signed in 1876, was one of a series of treaties that the nascent government of Canada signed with indigenous leaders in the 1870s; the treaties were intended to prepare the way for settlement. The Stoney Knoll Reserve, however, had been reallocated by the Canadian government in the late 1890s. The government, looking for farmland for settlers, argued that the Young Chippewayan appeared to be disbanded and the land unoccupied. They then opened it for settlement, which included providing a large block of land to newcomer Mennonite farmers, from whom some of the 1976 farmers had descended. The government, however, had acted without surrender or approval by the Young Chippewayan as was required by the Treaty, and so had broken Treaty law.

One hundred years after the signing of Treaty Six, when the car visited the farms, descendants and others familiar with the Young Chippewayan claim, were acting upon their frustration that this land had been taken. For their part, the Young Chippewayan had left the area due to lack of food, the failure of the government to provide farming implements as promised in order to make farming possible, as well as disease and death—including the death of their chief who had signed the treaty. In order to survive, families had moved and joined with other bands although they were not recognized as members of these other bands. Young Chippewayan members remained landless and uncompensated.

Over the next two decades, the moral value landscape slowly began to change, as did the views of the conflict in good measure based on historical research: first by the consultant and then by a longer and more extensive government Commission report on the case in 1994. Together these documents helped settlers connected to the area understand the significance and legitimacy of the Young Chippewayan claim. It provided vital information that prompted people to rethink the conflict and their values vis-à-vis the conflict.

Another element that helped to reframe the situation was utopian thinking. A key Young Chippewayan interlocutor, when thinking about what a good future would look like, asked Mennonites in the area to stand with the Young Chippewayan in their claim to the government and not to feel threatened. He emphasized that the Young Chippewayan wanted their claim justly addressed but were not asking for the Stoney Knoll land. In so doing, he foregrounded the moral good of relationality as integral to the process of addressing the land claim. This call was taken up by Mennonite interlocutors, who worked at raising awareness and suggested the same reframing in their calls to action: solidarity and responsiveness to genuine need and exclusion. The larger religious denominational body and affiliated NGO, to which many of the farmers were connected, increasingly formulated these moral values in public statements that utilized restorative justice language.

Nevertheless, frustrations on both sides of the conflict in the Laird area persisted for over two decades. The legal claims process was exceedingly slow for members of the Young Chippewayan, and it framed their claim and connections to the area in win-lose terms for band members. The farmers in the area were frustrated as they felt their livelihoods and connections to the area threatened. The less tangible sense of identifying with that particular area of land in the Saskatchewan valley—land on which ancestors had lived and toiled—was also a source of tension on both sides.

Over time, the moral values of care and relationality as well as just or fair treatment of all individuals gained traction. There was also an increased valuing of action, individual agency, and responsiveness to the problem as part of contributing to restorative justice and collective flourishing. In 2006, an event was held at Stoney Knoll to commemorate the 130th anniversary of the signing of Treaty Six. Some 130 people, including Young Chippewayan members as well as Mennonite and Lutheran farmers from the area, came together in a day-long ceremony that included a pipe ceremony, prayers, eating, dancing, singing, a presentation on treaties, and an exchange of gifts. It also involved the signing of a Memorandum of Understanding that indicated communities would respect the Treaty and work together to pursue peace, justice, and self-sufficiency. Cumulatively, the day offered an act of solidarity that committed those who lived in the area to support the Young Chippewayan in their on-going struggle for recognition, as well as a chance to meet and establish relationships that could create a broader foundation for moving forward in relation to the conflict and respond to the issues at hand.

The Young Chippewayan legal claim continues to be unresolved, requiring detailed genealogical work from the late nineteenth century. There continue to be events to raise awareness about the Young Chippewayan situation, for example another gathering was held at Stoney Knoll in 2011. In 2015, the fifth annual Spruce River Folk Fest was held, a now yearly event intended to raise awareness about landless bands, particularly the Young Chippewayan, which is hosted by one of the former farmer-residents of the area. The annual Folk Fest also helps raise funds to support the genealogical research project. Finally, there are some efforts to rethink possible land-related solutions beyond the government's legal Treaty claims process.

In retrospect, background research opened space for creative thinking and moved the parties toward longer-term peacebuilding and reconciliation. Utopian thinking, offered by a Young Chippewayan representative, enabled actors to rethink the presenting problems through a relational lens. Relational ethics, in turn, have generated a rich set of responses that have added to the initial considerations of duty and consequences. Valuing relationships and responsiveness to those with whom one is in relationship has transformed the conflict into a collaborative effort to address historical wrongs around land claims.

CONCLUSION

It is a challenge to ensure that there is space for open, careful, and creative thinking about moral values and identifying ethical actions, particularly when they are tied to value conflicts within an organization, between members of the same peacebuilding team or between different stakeholders, institutions, and departments—from government to military actors, from national to local actors, from external to internal actors. Finding creative ways to meet multiple values in Afghanistan's NSP, for example, took open, careful, and creative thinking that bridged a series of stakeholders and benefited from case comparison. In Stoney Knoll, research combined with utopian thinking helped move a farming community to reprioritize its moral values, and in so-doing has been integral to community responsiveness and action to transform the conflict. These are just some of the ways that creative problem-solving can help move practitioners and stakeholders beyond mental blocks, self-justification, and dogmatism in the midst of rapid decision-making in field work and conflict environments.

It is important to recognize, however, that while we are each moral agents, we also operate within groups and teams. Our agency or ability to act ethically is shaped, supported, and inhibited by the norms and structures in which we find ourselves. To maintain and foster space for open, careful, *and* creative thinking, requires not only developing individual skills in moral analysis and attention to moral values, but also attending to the dynamics of decision-making on teams, in organizations, and institutions. How, then, do we develop work environments that support creative ethical thinking to inform action? It is to this challenge that we turn next.

FOR FURTHER EXPLORATION

Here are some questions and activities that you can use to further think about issues raised in this chapter:

- Have you ever been in a situation where your values conflicted in peacebuilding work? How did you respond? Were there better ways to respond?
- What creative problem-solving techniques do you prefer to use? How have these helped you?
- Choose one of the following scenarios. Apply one (or more) of the creative problem-solving methods. Come to a decision about your course of action.

  Scenario 1: You work for a peacebuilding and development organization that has been operating in-country for about fifteen years. You are currently in charge of operations. Your organization has offices in two urban centers—the drive between the offices takes about five hours. One of the urban centers is on the brink of extensive fighting as the hostilities between the combatant groups are being renewed. A two-year ceasefire agreement has broken down and security sources report the groups are heavily armed and beginning to move into the urban area from their respective encampments. Your organization is debating whether or not to evacuate staff members from the conflict-affected area. You know that the presence of your organization is important to local community members—they have told you that your presence has helped to deter violence, and that your ability to broadcast information to multiple sides of the conflict has helped defuse violence and prevented false rumors from producing violence and massive displacement in one area. You are also concerned that your seven staff members are at risk and jeopardizing their lives by staying in the office. You have done a risk assessment and know that while you can mitigate some of the risks to staff, you cannot guarantee they will be safe. What are the values at stake in this decision? What are your options? How will you decide? What will you decide?

Scenario 2: You are a member of a small peacebuilding organization of five members. A rebel leader has asked to meet with you and two of your team members. The leader has not provided a reason for why he is requesting the meeting. There are rumors that the leader wants to negotiate a zone of peace in a region that has seen heavy fighting in recent days (despite the national ceasefire). Several organizations have had members taken hostage for hefty ransom payments in the past year in this same area. It is not clear whether the hostages were taken by the rebel group or another group also in the area. Do you agree to travel to meet with the rebel leader? What are the values at stake in this decision? What are your options? How will you decide? What will you decide?

Scenario 3: You are a peacebuilder with an organization that wants to do a "training of trainers." You are part of the team that is to set up the trainings that will involve youth leaders, teachers, elders, and key government officials in communities that have flash points, where conflicts frequently re-erupt. The organization with which you work has set a policy that people who participate in the trainings will not receive per diems, as they believe it is a disincentive to genuine participation. They see a pattern that people simply go from one training to another without implementing anything. When you go to recruit trainees, potential participants repeatedly ask about the amount of per diems that will be paid by the organization. The government officials and elders consistently indicate they will not participate without per diems. People within your organization are divided. Some think that the most important thing is that the training happens and key people are there, regardless of how they get there. Others think that if people are only coming for the money, then nothing will get done anyway after the training so no point including people. Another colleague thinks that the organization's policy is wrong, and it is very important to compensate people for their time as they would otherwise be generating income. What are the values at stake in this decision? What are your options? How will you decide? What will you decide?

- Identify a critical, values-based problem in current peacebuilding work—this could be your own work, or one you develop based upon news reports. Engage in creative problem solving to try to come up with possible moral responses and make a decision.

NOTES

1. Roger Fisher and William Ury's *Getting to Yes: Negotiating Agreement without Giving In* (second edition, New York: Penguin Books, 1991; third edition with Bruce Patton, New York: Penguin Books, 2011) provides a classic introduction to interest-based negotiation, upon which the updated 2011 version builds.
2. Michael Davis' article "The Moral Justifiability of Torture and Other Cruel, Inhuman, or Degrading Treatment" was published in 2005 (*International Journal of Applied Philosophy,* 19 (2):161–78).
3. For more ideas on creative thinking, a good resource is Michael Michalko's *Cracking Creativity: the Secrets of Creative Genius* (Berkeley, CA: Ten Speed Press, 2001). See also James Jaccard and Jacob Jacoby's *Theory Construction and Model-Building Skills: A Practical Guide for Social Scientists* (New York: Guilford Press, 2009).
4. For a discussion of the role of the moral imagination and positive visioning in peacebuilding see John Paul Lederach's book *The Moral Imagination: The Art and Soul of Building Peace* (New York: Oxford University Press, 2005). See also Elise Boulding's work *Building a Global Civic Culture: Education for an Interdependent World* (Syracuse, NY: Syracuse University Press, 1990).
5. For more on how dissent can be helpful in sparking creativity, see Charlan Nemeth's work, such as "Managing Innovation: When Less Is More" (*California Management Review*, 40(1):59–74, 1997). If you are interested in how group dynamics contribute to flawed thinking, read Irving Janis's now-classic *Groupthink* (second edition, Boston: Wadsworth Cengage Learning, 1982).
6. For an exploration of development agencies and their relationship to the genocide in Rwanda, see Peter Uvin's *Aiding Violence: The Development Enterprise in Rwanda* (West Hartford, CT: Kumarian Press, 1998).
7. For an early discussion of problem-solving workshops, see Herbert Kelman and Stephen Cohen's "The Problem-Solving Workshop: A Social-Psychological Contribution to the Resolution of Conflicts" (*Journal of Peace Research*, 13(2): 79–90, 1976), or for a more contemporary overview, see Ronald Fisher's edited volume *Paving the Way: Contributions of Interactive Conflict Resolution to Peacemaking* (Lanham, MD: Lexington Books, 2005).
8. International Alert has worked on a Code of Conduct: Conflict Transformation Work (London, UK: International Alert, 1998) to help inform professional standards in peacebuilding, and it can be used as professional input into making decisions when moral values conflict.

9. Peacebuilding dilemmas, such as those in Afghanistan, have been studied by a number of authors. Anna Jarstad, for example, identifies systemic and temporal dilemmas, among others, in her chapter "Dilemmas of War-to-Democracy Transitions: Theories and Concepts" in *From War to Democracy: Dilemmas of Peacebuilding*, edited by Anna K. Jarstad and Timothy D. Sisk (New York: Cambridge University Press, 2008). See also Chuck Call's edited volume with Vanessa Wyeth, *Building States to Build Peace* (Boulder, CO: Lynne Rienner Publishers, Inc., 2008). For more detailed examination of peacebuilding in Afghanistan, see Chuck Thiessen's *Local Ownership of Peacebuilding in Afghanistan* (Lanham, MD: Lexington Books, 2014) or Richard Ponzio's *Democratic Peacebuilding: Aiding Afghanistan and other Fragile States* (New York: Oxford University Press, 2011).

10. The case exploration of QIP and NSP draws on the following reports: Paul Fishstein and Andrew Wilder "Winning Hearts and Minds? Examining the Relationship between Aid and Security in Afghanistan" (Medford, MA: Feinstein International Center, 2012); Curt Tarnoff "Afghanistan: U.S. Foreign Assistance" (Washington, DC: Congressional Research Service, August 21, 2012); Daisaku Higashi's report "The Challenge of Constructing Legitimacy in Peacebuilding: Case of Afghanistan" (*CIR Working Paper No. 47*, Vancouver, British Columbia: Centre of International Relations, 2008); Jon Bennett, Jane Alexander, Douglas Saltmarshe, Rachel Phillipson, and Peter Marsden's *Country Programme Evaluation Afghanistan, Evaluation Report EV 696* (United Kingdom: Department for International Development [DFID], 2009); Action Aid, Afghanaid, Care Afghanistan, Christian Aid, Concern Worldwide, Norwegian Refugee Council, Oxfam International, and Trocaire's "Quick Impact, Quick Collapse: The Dangers of Militarized Aid in Afghanistan" (joint paper, 2010); Mark Ward's op-ed "Quick Impact Projects Slow Progress in Afghanistan." *The Boston Globe*, October 15, 2009); Inger W. Boesen, "From Subjects to Citizens: Local Participation in the National Solidarity Programme" (Kabul: Afghanistan Research and Evaluation Unit, 2004); Andrew Beath, Fontini Christia, and Ruben Enikolopov's "The National Solidarity Program: Assessing the Effects of Community-Driven Development in Afghanistan" (Policy Research Working Paper No. 7415; Washington, DC: World Bank Group, Office of the Chief Economist, East Asia and the Pacific Region, 2015); and Sultan Barakat (lead evaluator), "Mid-term Evaluation Report of the National Solidarity Programme (NSP), Afghanistan" (York, United Kingdom: Post-war Reconstruction & Development Unit (PRDU), The University of York, and Ministry of Rural Rehabilitation and Development, Islamic Republic of Afghanistan, 2006).

For further information on the development of the NSP idea and earlier experiences with a similar model in Indonesia, see Gregory Warner's article, "The Schools the Taliban Won't Torch" (*Washington Monthly*, 2007; available online at: http://www.washingtonmonthly.com/features/2007/0712.warner.html) and Scott Guggenheim's 2004 paper "Crises and Contradictions: Understanding the Origins of a Community Development Project in Indonesia" (Jakarta: World Bank). For a more positive review of PRTs, see Sharon Morris et al.'s interagency report "Provincial Reconstruction Teams in Afghanistan an Interagency Assessment" (Washington, DC: USAID, 2006). For a critique of the way in which moral values are being addressed in Afghanistan's NSP, see Alessandro Monsutti's article "Fuzzy Sovereignty: Rural Reconstruction in Afghanistan, between Democracy Promotion and Power Games" (*Comparative Studies in Society and History,* 54 (3):563–91, 2012).

11. There are a variety of sources that provide information on Stoney Knoll, the Young Chippewayan claim, and the community response. For background and the Canadian Crown arguments in the case, see the commission report by Carole Corcoran, Daniel Bellegarde, and James Prentice, *The Young Chippewayan Inquiry into the Claim Regarding Stoney Knoll Indian Reserve No. 107* (Ottawa, ON: Indian Claims Commission, 1994). The first report of the area produced for the faith-based non-governmental Mennonite organization in response to the visits was Leonard Doell's "History of the Mennonites and Natives in the Last One Hundred Years" (Saskatoon: Native Ministries, Mennonite Central Committee Canada, 1977). For more detail on the decade of responses within the community between 1977 and 1987, see chapter 5 of Reina Neufeldt's *Barn Razing: Change and Continuity in Identity during Conflict* (PhD doctoral dissertation, School of International Service, American University, 2005). Eric Olfert provides a participant response to the 2006 event in an article titled "Historic Meeting on Stoney Knoll" (*Intotemak* 35(3):1, 4). There are also some websites with additional documentation, such as the Blogspot Young Chippewayan website at: http://youngchippewayan.blogspot.ca/p/minnonite-reserve-as-part-of-young.html, and the Mennonite Central Committee Saskatchewan website at: http://mcccanada.ca/learn/more/stoney-knoll.

6

Nurturing Ethical Environments

ALONE

Edward Snowden grabbed news headlines around the world in 2013 when he revealed details of the U.S. National Security Agency program codenamed Prism, which included extensive monitoring of cell phone logs and Internet communication. Snowden stated in a note accompanying the first set of documents he provided to the *Guardian*, "'I understand that I will be made to suffer for my actions,' but 'I will be satisfied if the federation of secret law, unequal pardon and irresistible executive powers that rule the world that I love are revealed even for an instant'" (Greenwald et al., 2013). Snowden was an individual who felt he had to take a stand on a critical moral issue and had no other options. Some now hold Snowden up as a moral exemplar, a lone ranger who did what he had to do to make a grave violation of rights known. Others vilify Snowden for endangering American national security and leaking classified information. Snowden, like Bradley Manning or Julian Assange in recent years, gained notoriety for being a whistleblower.[1]

At one end of the spectrum, the term whistleblower conjures up images of a referee in a game, who whistles a play down after a foul has been committed. Here the connotation is positive. The referee is playing an important role in ensuring the game is played fairly and follows the rules. Whistleblowers are simply doing the right thing and whistling down a foul play. A whistleblower who needs protection is someone who has no other recourse than taking extraordinary action in order to raise up or address current wrongs. Whistleblower protection legislation is therefore enacted in many countries to protect people who report acts of wrongdoing in order to ensure their employers do not retaliate against them.

The need for protection speaks to how people view whistleblowers on the other end of the spectrum. Here the term whistleblower carries with it very negative connotations. Whistleblowers are seen as people who betray the trust of an organization, who "squeal" on colleagues, who are seen to be pursuing a personal vendetta or interested in being famous. When whistleblowing is viewed from this perspective, it is seen as a threat to team conformity and unity and carries costs, such as exclusion, demotions, reduced funding, retaliation, or prison sentences.

In Snowden's situation, he states emphatically that he did not have recourse to whistleblower protections as a member of the intelligence community. He argues that if there were stronger whistleblower protections in place, "If we had had a real process in place, and reports of wrongdoing could be taken to real, independent arbiters rather than captured officials, I might not have had to sacrifice so much to do what at this point even the president seems to agree needed to be done" (Gabbatt, 2014). Snowden also rejects being characterized as either a traitor or a hero. In a 2015 interview, he responded, "I reject both [labels] because even though people say being a hero would be a good thing, it's other-izing, it's distancing, it's, 'This person did something I could never do in that situation'—that's absolutely not true" (McCarthy, 2015). Recent U.S. court decisions suggest that the prism program was indeed illegal.

The very phenomenon of whistleblowing—whether protected or not—speaks to group moral failure and highly problematic ethical environments. Going public with details that will shame and legally implicate an organization means that no other avenue to address moral concerns was available or working. Legal provisions for whistleblowing are laudable in that they create a legal avenue for people to go outside of regular channels when identifying and naming moral failures. Moral courage in individuals who stand up for moral values is important *and at the same time* we need to do better at ensuring work and group environments are themselves ethical. This requires identifying, processing, and responding to moral concerns and failings as they happen.

There are two pieces of the puzzle here that require attention. One is with respect to individual moral agency and the other is with respect to group dynamics and the ethical environment in which we work (see figure 6.1). This chapter explores both the power of personal choices as well as the importance of developing healthy ethical organizations to ensure we are doing the best we can. We will begin, however, with an exploration of what goes wrong—what inhibits or constrains moral behavior in groups.

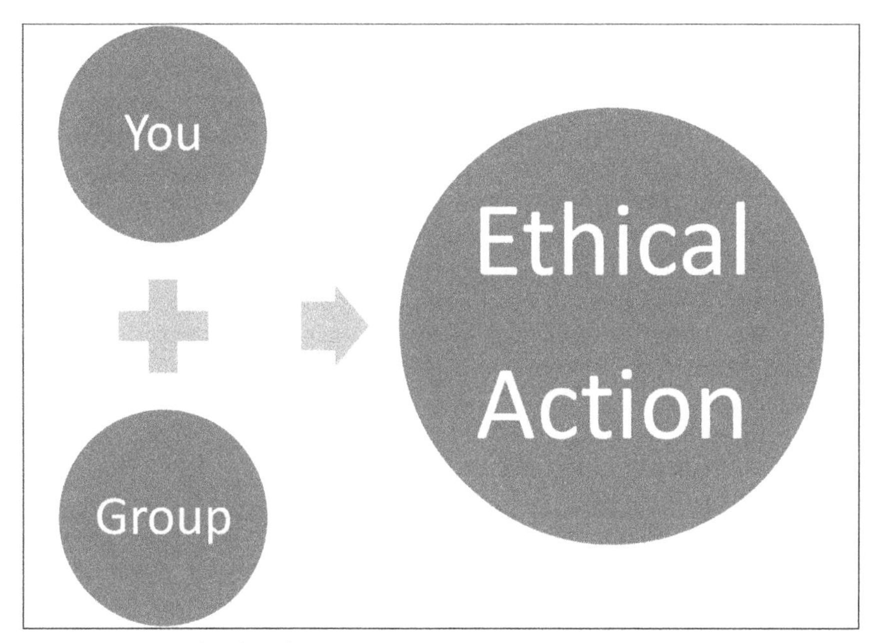

Figure 6.1. An Ethical Action Equation

CONSTRAINTS ON MORAL BEHAVIOR IN GROUPS

Often our worst behavior arises from within groups. In some situations, this occurs because we have abrogated our role as moral agent and passed on the power to make moral decisions to leaders. In other situations, it occurs because of more subtle group dynamics that occur, particularly in settings where people are under duress. The group may be physically present in that we are sitting with group members in a meeting room, or the group might affect us in terms of shaping how we think about and interact with those around us even when group members are not physically present.

A relatively minor but clear example of my own, when I made a poor ethical choice because of a faulty perception of my role within an organization, may help to ground the discussion of group failure in everyday situations. There was a moment when I made a poor decision about where to place myself in a community meeting in Dili when political leaders were present. The meeting was in a local "hotspot" and part of an effort to diffuse tensions. I seated myself obviously in the front row in order to make myself and my organization visible in response to pressures I felt for branding. I soon regretted that choice because of the unintentional messages that my foreigner presence sent to others at the meeting regarding outsider roles in insider processes. In many ways it undercut the very purpose of the meeting and our organizational intentions. For some reason, in that moment, I made a poorly considered choice based upon what I thought was being asked of me. With more time to think about the choice, I would have realized two things: first, this was likely not what my organization was actually asking for regarding recognition; and second, even if it was, had I raised questions of possible harms that might result my colleagues would have been receptive to those concerns. I unwittingly constrained my choices and assumed a stance that short-circuited fulsome discussion of an issue that needed attention.

We have many twentieth- and twenty-first-century examples of significantly more dramatic and horrific group moral failings. These range from Canada's residential school system that was designed to "make white" indigenous peoples; to World War II Nazi extermination camps; to the Tuskegee syphilis experiments; to the authorized use of torture and rape as weapons of war; and the list goes on. While we might like to blame these failings on particular people whom we name as morally depraved, individuals act with the tacit consent of those around them and are enabled by the structures that support particular types of behavior as acceptable. The pictures of soldiers abusing prisoners in Iraq's Abu Ghraib prison that were taken as personal mementos speak to the failure of not just the individuals who were charged and found guilty, but also of the larger moral failure of military culture and decisions around the authorized use of "enhanced interrogation techniques." The same dynamic occurred in the other situations mentioned as well, and while individuals are culpable and make decisions as unique moral agents, the group environment in which we make decisions is important and significantly affects decisions. This dynamic brings us back to Hannah Arendt, and her observation (noted at the beginning of the book) with respect to individuals like Adolf Eichmann who may be limited in their ability to think morally. Arendt recognized the importance and banality of the bureaucratic environment in which Eichmann was located that enabled evil to occur without question.

Craig Johnson, a professor of leadership studies and expert in organizational ethics, identifies at least five group processes and dynamics drawn from social psychology that contribute to group moral failure in organizations: groupthink, mismanaged agreement, escalating commitment, excessive control, and moral exclusion. Each of these may occur in peacebuilding and are briefly defined in textbox 6.1, with greater exploration of moral exclusion and groupthink after the textbox due to their relevance for peacebuilding.[2]

Groupthink and moral exclusion are particularly relevant to people working in conflict-affected contexts due to the pressures of the context and the nature of the dehumanizing elements of conflict. It is therefore worth examining both in greater depth to facilitate their recognition as well as to help identify ways to respond.

TEXTBOX 6.1. PROBLEMATIC GROUP DYNAMICS

Groupthink: When groups or teams make a faulty decision because they prioritize group cohesion; group pressures lead to a deterioration of reality testing, mental efficiency, and moral judgment. Identified by social psychologist Irving Janis in 1972.

Mismanaged agreement or the Abilene paradox: When a group or team goes along with a decision they don't like because no one expresses public opposition to it. Everyone therefore appears to agree, even though they do not. Like the family who drove to Abilene for a meal that no one wanted, no one wants to "rock the boat." Identified by Jerry Harvey in 1974.

Escalating commitment: When an individual or team increases its efforts and adds resources to try to make things go right when things go wrong. Rather than cutting costs or changing courses of action, they continue to try to make things right because they feel responsible, cognitively distort negative information and misguidedly believe they can change things. A dynamic initially studied by Eliott Aronson, Barry Staw, and others in the 1960s and 1970s.

Excessive or concertive control: When self-directed groups or teams with a common set of values, high levels of coordination, and self-generated reinforcement mechanisms exert powerful control over group members; James Barker (1993) argues that this type of control can lead to a Weberian iron cage of rationality if not managed well.

Moral exclusion: When individuals, teams, or large-scale groups intentionally exclude others (usually connected to an identity group classification) from the category of being a human and deserving of basic moral respect, justice, or fairness. A phenomenon studied by Morton Deutsch (1990) as well as Susan Opotow (1990), among others, in social and educational psychology.

As noted, groupthink was a term coined by social psychologist Irving Janis (1972), and it occurs when a group makes faulty decisions because group pressures lead to a deterioration of "mental efficiency, reality testing, and moral judgment" (p. 9). Janis developed the term after analyzing U.S. decision-making procedures connected to foreign policy disasters, like the failed invasion of Cuba known as the Bay of Pigs fiasco. Groups affected by groupthink ignore alternatives and tend to take irrational actions that dehumanize other groups. Groups are particularly vulnerable to this dynamic when their members have similar backgrounds, they are insulated from outside opinions (e.g., private meetings or dealing with secure information), when it is not clear what rules a decision-making process will follow, when there are highly directive leaders as well as pressure to come to a decision. Part of the dynamic is that team members value unanimous agreement and group cohesiveness over open and reasoned problem-solving.

Janis identified a series of symptoms of groupthink that group members can be alert to in order to recognize if it is occurring. Symptoms cluster in three categories, the first of which involves overestimating the group's capacities, which includes over-confidence among group members, an illusion of invulnerability, and belief in the inherent morality of the group itself. A second set of symptoms cluster around closed-mindedness in discussions, which involves discounting warnings as the group rationalizes its decisions, and regular use of stereotypes of outsiders in discussions. The third set of symptoms relate to pressures toward uniformity, and there is evidence of increased self-censorship, the appearance of group unanimity in their thinking even if there is not, a pressure on dissenters not to dissent, and the presence of self-appointed "mind guards" who prevent counter-information or problematic, negative information from affecting the leader and group. To avoid groupthink, peacebuilders can watch for these symptoms in meeting discussions, particularly as plans of action are developed which can lead to ill-advised peacebuilding strategies.

The process of moral exclusion is tied to dehumanization, which is prevalent in deeply divided societies. Moral exclusion is therefore highly central to conflict resolution and peacebuilding processes. Our worst human atrocities occur when we exclude others from the boundaries of those who deserve to be treated as morally human. It is when we consider others as no longer deserving of moral treatment that torture and genocide become morally justified, because these are not people we are attacking; they are "dogs" (as in Abu Ghraib in 2003), they are "cockroaches" or "snakes" (in Rwanda in 1994), or "rats" (as in Jews in Germany during World War II). This is not a past phenomenon; the current discussion of how to treat Syrian refugees and respond to the recent Islamic State–linked terrorist attacks in Lebanon, Egypt, and Paris deploys discourse that suggests moral exclusion is occurring.

Susan Opotow has identified five elements of moral exclusion. One is that conflicts of interest are salient and appear to be win–lose (for example, "our lives" or "your lives" in settings of escalating conflict or full-out war). A second feature is that identity group categorizations are highly salient or relevant, such as along national or religious lines (e.g., during World War II, being Japanese in Canada or the United States meant you went into an internment camp). A third element of moral exclusion is that moral justifications for the exclusion are prominent; groups determine that they are morally right in taking action to protect themselves against an unjust and inhumane other/enemy. A fourth element of moral exclusion is that unjust procedures are accepted as being an expedient way to achieve a greater good, even though they might not be the best. Finally, harmful outcomes are accepted as part of the process, providing that the harm is directed to others.

Peacebuilders work in contexts marked by moral exclusion and dehumanization. Tim Murithi, in his book *The Ethics of Peacebuilding,* argues that one of the central tasks of peacebuilding is to address the problem of moral exclusion. Transforming moral communities to include former enemies is a central challenge that is both a feature of how we work and an end we may pursue through our work.[3]

CONFORMITY AND OBEDIENCE

Two threads running through these different types of faulty group dynamics relate to conformity and obedience. Much of our peacebuilding work occurs in teams or with large groups of people. When we work with people, cooperation and coordination are important. This sometimes means that our own individual ideas and perspectives are suppressed in the interest of the group. This particularly happens when we feel we are working for a cause greater than ourselves and we feel committed to the values at stake in our work. While this is healthy and helps produce positive team cohesion and solidarity, it can lead to problems of obedience and conformity if we are not careful—which speaks to the negative side of group cohesion and the specter of collective moral failing.

Conformity and obedience pose real problems for ethical peacebuilding practice. Studies in social psychology, like the Stanford prison experiments or Stanley Milgram's now infamous studies of conformity, show how even in an experiment where the stakes for non-conformity are low, we have a tendency to turn off our own moral compass and defer moral decisions to others who we see as being in authority.[4] In Stanley Milgram's famous experiments on obedience, participants (young male college students at Yale) believed they were taking part in a study of learning that involved administering shocks to another individual (who was not actually receiving shocks, but was an actor for the purposes of the experiment). In the first experiment, some 60 percent of participants administered the maximum shock level to another person despite dramatic red warning signs on the dial regarding the negative effects on the person, as well as the screams of pain coming from the "learner" who was in another room and had also complained of a heart condition. This acquiescence occurred as an "expert" in a lab coat close at hand exhorted them to continue with the study. Sixty percent of the participants administered the maximum 450 volts on the dial despite exhibiting their own distress signs, such as protesting, nervous laughter, and even crying. The results disturbingly suggested that people conform to the expectations of those in authority, and frequently obey when others, who appear to know more or are willing to take moral responsibility for the decision, tell us to do something. It is a deeply disturbing finding regarding obedience.

Philip Zimbardo's Stanford prison experiment similarly demonstrated that people obey authority and conform to role expectations surprisingly quickly. In his experiment, students were randomly assigned to be prisoners or prison guards. They quickly conformed to those roles in surprising ways, as did the experiment team members themselves. Prisoners became a number instead of having a unique identity as their heads were shaved and other intake procedures turned them into inmates. Prison guards wore glasses that ensured they possessed anonymity in interactions with the prisoners. Zimbardo, the lead researcher, responded to outsider questions many times as if he was a prison official rather than a researcher. The two-week experiment was stopped six days in, after guards began acting in sadistic ways and prisoners became depressed and showed signs of extreme stress. As with the Milgram experiments, the stakes for conformity and obedience were low because participants were students who were randomly assigned to groups, and yet they developed very disturbing patterns of behaviors.

Bad things—actions that went against people's morals and moral character—started to happen simply due to the simulation conditions in both Milgram and Zimbardo's studies. The powerful social situations they created, which involved both conformity to role expectations and obedience to a perceived authority, produced outcomes in behavior that surprised many people at the time (these studies have also gained notoriety as examples displaying questionable research ethics, because of the negative effects on participants). Warning signs of work environments in which moral decision-making may be inhibited or constrained mirror the problematic group dynamics noted above. They include strong pressures for conformity to the group, failing to reconsider initial commitments even when there are good reasons for so doing, treating outsiders less ethically than insiders, and telling unethical stories as a point of pride amongst coworkers.

Given the challenges to moral and ethical thinking connected to group dynamics and pressures of conformity and obedience, how do we respond? How can we ensure that we support ethical individual choices and environments in which ethical questions are asked, valued, and deliberated upon in order to avoid problematic group processes?

THE COURAGE TO ACT

One part of the response equation (figure 6.1) is with respect to individual action, and the courage to act based on one's moral values. Whistleblowers such as Snowden demonstrate that they have the courage to act. Rushworth Kidder, who founded the Institute for Global Ethics in 1990, authored a book called *Moral Courage* (2006) in which he defines moral courage as "the quality of mind and spirit that enables one to face up to ethical challenges firmly and confidently" (p. 72). He suggests that people who act based on moral courage are able to apply their moral values in daily life, assess risk or danger within situations, and nevertheless display a willingness to endure hardship and act upon important values. Moral courage, he suggests, is necessary when there might be negative consequences for right actions. The dangers or negative consequences might range from verbal to online and media attacks, from unpopularity to losing support, being excluded, sued, or even threatened with physical harm.[5]

Kidder also suggests there are some things that regularly inhibit moral courage, which we need to address. A refusal to take responsibility or indecisiveness can prevent people from taking action. Being sensitive to criticism and a desire to be accepted can also inhibit moral courage—responses which are noted above as part of what feeds problematic group dynamics, such as groupthink and mismanaged agreement. Further, Kidder also names indifference and shamelessness as possible barriers to moral courage, which relate to personal moral character development as well as the idea that shame is a positive response to social expectation that helps us live together well.

When I ask people to name others whom they see as moral exemplars, they often respond with examples of very famous people who exhibit moral courage—people like Malala Yousafzai, Mother Theresa, Mahatma Gandhi, Martin Luther King Jr., Bacha Khan, Dorothy Day, Nelson Mandela, or the Dalai Lama. All are heroes to whom we can all look for their extraordinary commitment to moral values. They have made choices based on their moral values and have stood fast in the face of immense pressure and antagonism, displaying abundantly the virtue of moral courage. They are indeed wonderful exemplars. Yet, as Snowden's quote alludes to regarding "othering," sometimes when we look *only* at the most extraordinary people, we undermine ourselves and our ability to engage in moral behavior. We look at these moral heroes and think it is impossible to do what they did. It is a bit like we are trying to imagine ourselves competing with Olympic athletes without sufficient training and preparation. If we fail to achieve what they did, it does not mean that we should give up on sports or morality all together. It might, however, suggest we need more training.

Another group of people respond to this question with what I call everyday moral exemplars. These are family members, friends, coworkers, teachers, or supervisors, who act as more intimate, daily moral guides. Everyday moral exemplars provide people with concrete models of how individuals can be ethical in their everyday life. These everyday exemplars often also display moral courage, and act based upon their values despite risks. They are also accessible figures to those naming them, and their moral feats appear more achievable. I think of a former work supervisor, who consistently acted in ways that embodied his ethical commitments even in a demanding work environment, who provides me with a good model of how to act. To return to the sports metaphor, these everyday exemplars are like local sports figures with whom we interact, watch, and play games, and from whom we learn in our everyday lives to improve our game.

In the section that follows, there is an example of a moral analysis that was done by an individual in the heat of the moment; it is an example of an everyday moral exemplar engaging in ethical reflective practice and demonstrating moral courage. The example itself is presented as a reproduction of a memo written by a peacebuilding staff member to senior managers in order to explore the moral dimensions of an organization's response to a vehicle collision. The collision occurred in the midst of an emergency humanitarian and peacebuilding initiative in the early stages of the response.

The memo is presented in detail because it is insightful both in terms of the content regarding the dilemma—which involves exploring how best to respond to the accident between a motorcycle driver and a larger vehicle—as well as the structure that the response took. In this case, an individual within an organization felt he was not being heard and that it was important for the organization to take a more informed and better moral stand on the problem. To get the attention of decision-makers in the organization he wrote-up a full analysis. While the staff member wrote the memo on his own, the content and his thinking was informed by opinions and voices of his local team members and community gatekeepers, which is similar to the values consultation process discussed in chapter three. For our purposes, it is a great example of the way that moral values help to frame decisions and can improve action within an organization.

A WORKING EXAMPLE: THE COLLISION

The text that follows was a memo written by a peacebuilder who was working in a context that was not his own but engaging closely with a team of local peacebuilders who were from the area, and he had been in the country for a number of years. The team realized the negative effects a decision regarding a response to an accident was having on their work with the community, and decided it was important for the peacebuilder to take action. Within the memo, in square brackets, you will see inserted notes about the moral perspective being deployed in the analysis to connect the example to the moral theories discussed in chapter 4.

The Case of the Accident: Perspectives and Recommendations to Management

Our organization is in a controversial situation. The motor vehicle accident on Tuesday between one of our drivers and a motorbike driver remains unresolved and is becoming a big issue that is regularly discussed amongst local staff and in the community. If it is not resolved, it will damage our reputation and status in the community where we work and live. As a senior advisor, I would like to offer the following analysis with a concluding recommendation.

Our Organization's Perspective—*While we are concerned about injured persons and our own employee and want to be sensitive to local perspectives on how to handle incidences like the above, our first response is to follow our policies. We are entitled to protect the organization and therefore prefer to act according to what is considered legally correct. In this case, management would like to see a proper police investigation that establishes who was right and who was wrong in the accident. If our driver is determined to be at fault, then our insurance will cover the costs of the injured persons and vehicle damage. However, we cannot assume liability and therefore cannot be expected to support the family financially without the police determining who was at fault. We do not want to enter into a negotiation process that might set a precedent for future claims of compensation and therefore would prefer to follow a legal procedure to protect our organization* [rule-based consequentialist thinking].

A Local Perspective—*In an accident like the above, it is understood that the person driving the bigger vehicle must take responsibility for the accident and for those injured as well as any damage sustained. The onus is on the driver of the bigger vehicle to drive in such a manner that those smaller vehicles and passengers will not come to harm* [duty to protect the vulnerable from harm]. *After the incident, the most important thing is the health and life of the people involved. We are therefore expected to show concern and to come to the assistance of the injured and support the family. The typical and preferred way is for the two parties to enter into negotiations to discuss the* *costs, then identify who pays for it and how to repair the vehicle damage. If the two parties reach an agreement, then it is formalized through the signature of the local leader, and the police will formally stamp such an agreement. The matter is then between the two parties and the police will release the vehicle and driver. If the parties cannot agree, then the police will keep the driver in custody and the vehicle in their compound*

Legal/Police Perspective*—The driver is being kept in custody, but is given permission to go home at night. He can be released under two conditions. The first is that the organization and the injured person's family agree to solve the matter between them. The second is that two or three other persons "stand good" for the driver—this means that if the driver would run away, then these people will be put in jail in his place. The police will do the investigation as requested by our organization and will hand the case over to the courts. The judge will make a final decision. If our driver is guilty, he will get a jail sentence. The family does not get any compensation. If the driver is not guilty, he will be released, and the family does not get any compensation.*

Frameworks for Justice

Distributive justice*—In this framework of justice, the focus is on establishing who is right and who is wrong. The offender gets punished once found guilty. The process is typically legal, conducted by lawyers who gather evidence and present facts supported by witnesses. Objectivity is important. A judge makes a final determination of right and wrong. The focus of the process is on the offender, adhering to the rule of law, procedure and formality. The process effectively excludes the broader community and is conducted (perhaps orchestrated) by experts. Decision-making is vested with a judge and not with the parties. Justice relates to establishing the "truth" about a past incident through investigation and presentation of facts.*

Our organization's approach in this instance falls in this paradigm of justice. We follow policy, want the police to investigate, have witnesses that support our case, and finally await a determination of who was at fault/was wrong before we will commit to paying any money. [Distributive justice here is undergirded by rule-based consequentialism.]

Restorative justice*—In this framework the focus is on re-establishing relationships. Justice is served when the parties can forgive each other, can live in harmony together, and can reconcile their differences and respect each other and the common values that bind them together. An injury or damage to one person is seen as an injury to the whole of the community, and the parties involved will be judged by the community as a whole in terms of their* *behavior and upholding agreed norms and values. The parties manage the process, and make the decisions and agreements. Justice is based on the future and how harmony is maintained between the parties and in the broader community.*

In the case of this accident, the negotiation on the surface is about the money and compensation. At a deeper level, the negotiation is about the building, reparation, and restoration of the relationship between our organization and the family of the injured, and more broadly between our organization and the wider community. We are seen as members of the community and are expected to behave as such. The emotional weight and assessment of injustice is on the side of the injured and the weaker party, in this case the motorbike driver and passenger, and we are judged in terms of our behavior after the incident and not whether the driver was technically correct in terms of traffic law. [Restorative justice here is undergirded by relational ethics].

Our Message to the Community

At the moment the message we are sending can be summarized as:

1. *Our own policy and procedures are more important than people or the community;*
2. *Legal rules take precedence over humanitarian and cultural norms;*
3. *Legal liability is more important than people's lives or health;*
4. *Our management is not willing to take responsibility when an incident such as this happens—no manager has been to the police, or has faced the family of the injured; and*
5. *We do not care for our employees.*

What is the message we want to send to the community about who we are and what we value?

1. *We are part of the community.*
2. *We respect the culture and norms of the society we live in.*
3. *We are a concerned humanitarian and peacebuilding organization.*
4. *We care for the communities we work in.*
5. *We care for and look after our employees.*

Potential Implications and Likely Consequences of Following a Distribute Justice Approach

- *The law (even if our driver is not guilty or at fault) will not protect us, our staff, and our property. We will be seen as outsiders and will be treated as such;*
- *Low morale will settle in amongst drivers because they are unsure of their safety and the support they will receive from management;*
- *Community retribution (e.g., damaging our vehicles, action against the driver, his family, and staff in vehicles);*

- *We will lose our identity as a respected organization when community leaders speak against us and when people see us as not respecting people, cultural norms, and community expectations; and*
- *Local staff (who are respected in the community) are undermined in the eyes of the local community, and their ability to play a constructive role in society is diminished.*

A Suggestion to Move Forward

1. *Trust local staff with local knowledge to take the lead with management's guidance (i.e. give a mandate to enter into negotiations with the families of the injured persons).*
2. *Get legal and local advice as to the expected outcome of an investigatory approach and court case—the risks are high.*

We have an experienced mediator on staff who has handled many cases like this in his role as a religious leader. He is trusted by the community for his fairness and respected for his integrity. At the moment, we are placing him in an impossible position by asking him to explain and defend a policy that is contrary to the values he knows and lives. He is placing his reputation and integrity at risk and soon will no longer be able to perform the role we are asking from him.

My suggestion is to give our staff member an open mandate—with guidelines—to act as facilitator between our organization and the family of the injured. It can be phrased that we are a humanitarian organization who is concerned for the family, and as part of the community, we would like to make a contribution to the costs associated with the transport and medical fees for the victims of the accident. Liability for the accident is still pending a police investigation, and for insurance and policy reasons, we need to pursue the legal route at the same time. Certain limits can be set—such as supporting the family for direct medical and transport expenses up to a certain maximum. Payment of this money does not in any way imply that the organization or driver is liable for the accident, but it is done purely out of human concern, to show our goodwill and to respect relationships and community values.

We will lose if we exclusively follow the legal route. Even if the investigation determines that our driver is not guilty from a technical point of view, we will be guilty from a local perspective and will be judged as having failed the community.

Based upon the staff members' analysis, managers within the organization referred to above switched tactics. It is an example of how someone acted with moral courage; he did not act entirely on his own, but he did work to counter problematic higher-management decision-making dynamics. As an interlocutor, the international peacebuilder was attuned to moral values and the relationship between moral values and the problematic decisions. He expanded on the context and facts in the case, carefully framed the issues, and analyzed them for his international colleagues drawing upon multiple moral values. He provided more than one possible scenario to compare possible lines of action. He also provided concrete and creative alternatives. These features expanded the space for and content of ethical deliberation (see textbox 6.2). In so doing, the everyday moral exemplar disrupted a problematic dynamic and shifted the conversation and action within the organization, which in turn shaped subsequent responses to the community.

Some peacebuilders will say that this example is about being conflict sensitive and that we have a moral imperative to be conflict sensitive. At one level, it is an example that reflects good practice, and that to which we are already attuned. Yet, being conflict sensitive may or may not mean being attuned to the moral value underpinning peacebuilding work and the choices we make therein (e.g., with whom we work, how we respond to hardliners). Process-wise, this is an example of someone who was attuned to values but not someone assigned to be an "ethics monitor" or internal ombudsperson. He was an attentive reflective practitioner who paid attention to values and its affects upon work, and was committed to doing good in a way that contributed to restorative justice. It made a difference.

TEXTBOX 6.2. FEATURES OF AN EVERYDAY MORAL EXEMPLAR'S ETHICS INTERVENTION

- Provided additional context information;
- Explored different perspectives on the problem (e.g., the views of the community, the staff, management, the injured party);
- Understood and applied multiple moral values (relational ethics, duty, consequences);
- Compared alternative responses thoughtfully;
- Generated an alternative course of action that met multiple values; and
- Connected questions and analysis to practical action.

ENHANCING ETHICAL TEAMS AND WORKPLACES

The other part of the equation depicted in figure 6.1 is, of course, the larger group, team, or work environment (which may or may not have fixed boundaries around it). While we need people to have moral courage, we also want to have workplaces where ethical deliberation and morality are practiced consistently. The peacebuilding team, noted above in the collision example, worked to create space in their organization for greater ethical deliberation in order to achieve a more moral course of action. Whistleblowers do the same, although they need to go outside of the regular system.

Ethical peacebuilding requires meaningful space to reflect on moral values in the midst of action and work environments This means very deliberately creating space for reflective practices in order to hear critical questions, think creatively, and imagine a more moral set of responses. Setting up supportive or healthy workplace environments to enable effective ethical reflection action cycles is an important part of the equation, and brings us back to the focus of chapter 2 and doable ethics. Healthy ethical work environments not only tolerate questions but nurture and sustain ethical practices. Within supportive environments, people are able to raise questions without fear that they will be fired, labeled as a disruptive troublemaker, or lose their standing; they are playing a valuable role to enhance the group's ethical functioning.

Johnson's analysis of organizations provides insight into what is needed to signal and maintain a healthy ethical climate. He observes that this includes formal and informal elements of an organization's culture, where culture refers to the operating, shared meanings, norms, values, and assumptions within an organization. Peacebuilding organizations can consider these formal and informal elements in order to foster a healthy ethical organization culture.

Formal elements of an organizational culture that help to maintain its ethical health include its worker expectations, structure, value systems, as well as reward and evaluation systems (see textbox 6.3). First, organizational expectations of behavior should be that people, from top leaders through to support staff, consistently act in ethically sound ways and model the values that the organization espouses. For peacebuilding organizations, this often means modeling the values of addressing conflict positively (not avoiding conflict), and creating a supportive work environment in which people experience care.

Second, the organization's structure can and should include clear lines of accountability, where people are aware of their personal responsibility for making decisions and have input on ethical dilemmas. For example, an international organization that works with local partners on peacebuilding needs to be clear that their partnership coordinator is responsible for ensuring partnerships are formed and proceed based upon a set of moral values that are collaboratively developed with partner organizations; they will need to address the intersection of power and insider-outsider roles in decision-making, and ensure that those who are most directly affected by the intervention have greater voice and stake, including in the identification of and discussion of moral values and their application to program areas. A supervisor can check in on this aspect of the work portfolio, ask how it is going, look to help problem-solve if required, and include this moral value aspect when they evaluate staff. The organizational structure can also include processes to vet decisions, in which leaders encourage others within the organization to challenge perspectives to foster an environment of open questioning.

Third, value systems can be articulated in mission statements as well as in core values that guide an organization's operations. It may be helpful to develop a code of conduct or set of operating principles although, as noted earlier, codes of conduct or general principles do not replace open and careful thinking about how values apply in the midst of fieldwork. Principles may also need to be periodically reviewed and revised. The pre-identification of values can, however, aid in recognizing moral value tensions, the assessment of different courses of action, and creative problem-solving as explored in chapter 5.

A fourth feature of an organizational culture that can be developed is with respect to its reward and evaluation or assessment system. This will vary based upon the size and type of organization. The general idea that Johnson proposes is that organizations can recognize and reinforce good moral behavior as part of the regular assessment of job performance. Organizations can also establish processes that do not tolerate destructive behaviors, such as aggression, sexual harassment, disrespect, or rudeness in the workplace. The purpose of these processes would be to treat people well, be just and caring, and foster greater collective flourishing within the organization.

TEXTBOX 6.3. WAYS TO FORMALLY NURTURE A HEALTHY ETHICAL CLIMATE WITHIN AN ORGANIZATION

- Model consistent, ethically sound, and holistic commitments to ethics in the workplace;
- Develop structures that reinforce ethics (monitor and evaluate process as well as end goals; ensure people have authority and responsibility for making moral decisions);
- Develop clear value statements and commitments;
- Recognize and reward ethical behavior at work; and
- Do not tolerate destructive behaviors (e.g., aggression, sexual harassment, discrimination).

Informal elements of an organization's culture also help to maintain its ethical health. Johnson notes that these include language, informal norms, and rituals, as well as the stories we tell about our work and organizations. In terms of language, we can become more comfortable in using moral language in the workplace, and use that language to assess values, what is right and good. As was discussed in chapters 3 and 4, we can watch for moral values in our work and listen to how people talk about what constitutes good and right in peacebuilding work. We can also look to avoid the traps of dogmatism, rationalization, and relativism in the language of our work environment.

A second area to monitor relates to the informal norms and rituals of the workplace (see textbox 6.4). We can assess if the expectations that we have about how people should act support our formal values. For example, the organization's behavioral norms captured in the memo on the case of the accident, presented above, were in direct contradiction to the organization's own stated values of showing solidarity with those with whom they were working. The norms of the operating culture were not in line and needed to be rethought. Organizations also sometimes have rituals of initiation or rites of passage, which are not written down but are enacted. These rituals and rites can be assessed for their moral values, and if they are assessed poorly, they can be changed. For example, sometimes people engaged in peacebuilding work internationally tell stories about various experiences and exploits; they sit down at the end of a long day of work, and engage in a ritual of regaling each other with stories of things that occurred during their travels, like how they discovered fraud that time in a village, or the time when they did something no one else would do, or the time they were in danger while out on a field trip. Storytelling and reflection are important on the whole and are often used to process experiences, to deal with unexpressed personal trauma, or to make connections between people—these are times when the stories, or rather the storytelling process, reinforces positive norms. Yet, there also are times when the story-telling seems gratuitous, when it appears people are simply telling a story for its shock value, to convey their personal value of thrill-seeking, or to build up their credibility as a peacebuilder who has travelled the world, seen a lot, and therefore is part of the group. Telling stories just to valorize peacebuilders, justify oneself, or thrill-seeking reflect deeply problematic informal norms that can be part of international peacebuilding work environments.

A final area of informal organizational life relates to the stories we tell about our organization. We can listen to these stories, ask if they are moral stories, and if not, develop new stories that reflect our moral commitments. Here the focus is on organizational stories rather than the ones we tell about ourselves and our experiences. A good example of positive moral stories about organizations are ones in which organizations admit to wrongdoing and include how the organization has changed to address the problem. One of the moral stories I learned when working at Catholic Relief Services (CRS) was the story of how CRS reconfigured its understanding of justice and the connections between justice, conflict, and peace in development work after

TEXTBOX 6.4. WAYS TO INFORMALLY NURTURE A HEALTHY ETHICAL CLIMATE WITHIN AN ORGANIZATION

- Recognize and use moral language in the workplace;
- Assess informal norms, rituals, and behavior expectations for their ethical messages; and
- Assess organizational stories and tell moral stories.

its failures as an organization in Rwanda in 1994 and its failure in the period leading up to the genocide. The horrific genocide produced a period of tremendous shame and soul-searching for development organizations like CRS; they had failed to recognize the significance of the divisions and the ways in which aid played into divisions within Rwanda. The moral stories then were about recognizing complicity, failing, and the need to rethink and reorient the way they engaged in development work in conflict affected contexts in the mid-1990s. Rethinking, fortunately, did not just occur behind closed doors but became part of the organization's broader narrative of why CRS worked not only on relief and development but also included a justice and peace lens in its work.

Ethical workplaces rely on the people within them to establish clear decision-making procedures, to identify moral values, to address destructive be-

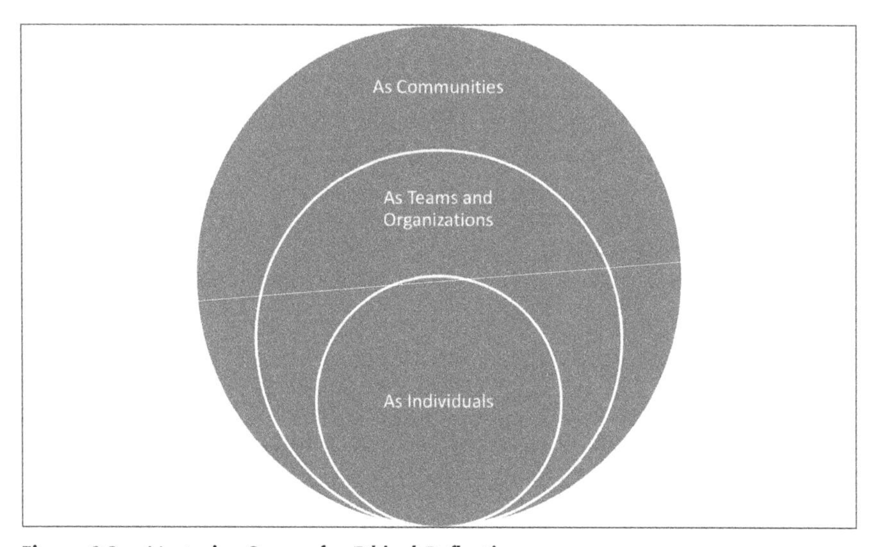

Figure 6.2. Nurturing Spaces for Ethical Reflection

haviors within the workplace, and to attend to the other formal and informal processes that can maintain a healthy ethical workplace. When we do this, we can avoid many of the problems of faulty group decision-making processes that contribute to moral failing, and the need for whistleblowers. That said, there still may be situations where pressures for group conformity or obedience produce problems. Being alert to moral values, as well as being willing to risk asking questions and raise issues that may cause conflict are important individual contributions that peacebuilders can make to their work environments. Peacebuilding requires moral courage and spaces for ethical reflection at multiple levels (see figure 6.2)—among individual peacebuilders, teams and organizations, and larger communities and systems—if peacebuilders are to confront moral exclusion and realize their potential to contribute to flourishing and good ends via right means.

FOR FURTHER EXPLORATION

Here are some questions and activities that you can use to further think about issues raised in this chapter:

- Are there times when you have felt pressured to conform to a particular moral decision with which you were uncomfortable? How did you deal with it? What else might you have done?
- If you currently work for an organization that engages in peacebuilding and conflict resolution, how healthy do you think the ethical climate is within your organization? What are some good features of the way the organization responds ethically? What are some areas the organization could improve?
- If you ran your own peacebuilding and conflict resolution organization, how could you ensure that the organization is ethically healthy? What formal and informal steps or measures could you undertake as a leader?
- What are some of the core values that you hold which you would also like to see the organization you work for hold?

NOTES

1. Edward Snowden's quote on why he released the NSA details is taken from the article "Edward Snowden: The Whistleblower Behind the NSA Surveillance Revelations," written by Glenn Greenwald, Ewen MacAskill, and Laura Poitras for *The Guardian* (online edition, June 10, 2013; available at: http://www.guardian.co.uk/world/2013/jun/09/edward-snowden-nsa-whistleblower-surveillance). His quote on

why he was unable to receive whistleblower protection comes from Adam Gabbatt's article, "'Not All Spying is Bad': Snowden Calls for Whistleblower Protection in Q&A" published in the *Guardian*, January 23, 2014. Available online at: http://www.theguardian.com/world/2014/jan/23/edward-snowden-nsa-whistleblower-courage-foundation. The third quote from Edward Snowden, noted above regarding his desire not to be other-ized, comes from a piece written by Tom McCarthy, called "Edward Snowden: Clinton Made 'False Claim' about Whistleblower Protection" (*Guardian*, October 16, 2015), which reported on a Skype-based interview Snowden gave at Bard College in New York and is available at: http://www.theguardian.com/us-news/2015/oct/16/edward-snowden-hillary-clinton-false-claim-whistleblower-protection.

2. The chapter draws on Craig Johnson's analysis of how to improve group ethical performance and create an ethical organization in *Ethics in the Workplace: Tools and Tactics for Organizational Transformation* (Thousand Oaks: Sage Publications, Inc., 2007). Irving Janis's concept of groupthink was explored in his book *Groupthink: Psychological Studies of Policy Decisions and Fiascos* (Boston, MA: Houghton Mifflin Company, 1982/1972). For more on escalating commitment, see Barry M. Staw, such as his early article "Knee-Deep in the Big Muddy: A Study of Escalating Commitment to a Chosen Course of Action" (*Organizational Behavior and Human Performance,* 16 (1):27–44, 1976). James Barker's analysis of the negative dimensions of concertive control are published in "Tightening the Iron Cage: Concertive Control in Self-Managing Teams" (*Administrative Science Quarterly,* 38:408–37, 1993). For further exploration of moral exclusion, see Susan Opotow's "Moral Exclusion and Injustice: An Introduction" and "Deterring Moral Exclusion" (both published in the *Journal of Social Issues,* 46 (1):1–20 and 173–82, 1990), or Morton Deutsch's "Psychological Roots of Moral Exclusion" (*Journal of Social Issues*, 46 (1):21–25, 1990).

3. For more, see Tim Murithi's *The Ethics of Peacebuilding* (Edinburgh: Edinburgh University Press Ltd., 2009). John Paul Lederach also indirectly addresses the importance of rebuilding a moral community in *The Moral Imagination* (New York: Oxford University Press, 2005).

4. Stanley Milgram's study of obedience is reviewed in his article "Behavioral Study of Obedience" (*The Journal of Abnormal and Social Psychology*, 67(4): 371–78, 1963), as well as his later book *Obedience to Authority* (New York: Harper & Row, 1974). The Stanford prison experiment was written up in a very readable format in "The Mind is a Formidable Jailer: A Pirandellian Prison," by Philip G. Zimbardo, Craig Haney, and Curtis Banks (*New York Times Magazine*, April 8, Section 6:38–60, 1973). There are also extensive images, discussion, and material from the experiment now available online at the website http://www.prisonexp.org/.

5. Rushworth Kidder's definition of moral courage comes from his book *Moral Courage* (New York: HarperCollins, 2005). In this book, he also explores the topics of learning moral courage and practicing moral courage in the public sphere.

7

Doing Good Well

Talking about the Real Issues

"We need to talk about the real issues," said a colleague who worked in Kosovo in 2000. He wondered aloud what should have been done when colleagues were out in the mountains in 1999, helping to pick up fleeing civilians, and young men who had clearly been fighters shortly before getting onto the aid trucks. The young men appeared to be looking for a temporary respite from the war in an internationally displaced persons (IDP) camp. His questions to us were: "What do you do? Do you take them on the trucks? Do you give them food?"

"Ethical issues come up around your own identity in working on peace . . . it is [the] decisions that come up that affect the way that you act as a peacebuilder in the situation, based on your identity. . . . I think it is an issue around what you represent and your identity. Irrespective of what cultural or religious group you're representing [whether American, Swedish or South African, Catholic or Muslim], you find yourself in different environments and who you are gets interpreted. It might damage your role . . . or it might help you."

"Our program has struggled with the questions: When and where does justice start, and when and how do we know that justice has come?"

"In this type of work you often sit down and have discussions with the parties, and you receive informal or privileged information that can be damaging to certain groups or people and you have to decide what to do with that information; that is something at a personal level, where you have to make decisions all the time. You have to make decisions, do you get into

favor with some people and share information that will help them, or do you not. That is a day-to-day decision. It matters. You want to be perceived by both sides positively, particularly if you are a negotiator, and it is a fine line. How do you deal with those situations and acknowledge your position without overstepping boundaries? How do you avoid favoritism?"

The above comments are from peacebuilding practitioners who raise some of the moral and ethical dilemmas they noticed in the midst of their everyday practice.[1] Peacebuilders encounter moral and ethical dilemmas all of the time. It is part of the nature of the work. Peacebuilding is a value-laden enterprise that involves encounters between and within moral communities. People typically engage in peacebuilding because they are motivated by moral values and want to do good, and yet peacebuilding can directly result in making things worse, for which we as peacebuilders are responsible. People can be harmed and killed as a direct or indirect result of our work. We can contribute to structural injustice. We can impose our values. We have been known to use people for our ends of advancement or stability. We can make poor choices, which reflect our personal vices, model poor ethics, and undermine collective flourishing. We can ignore needs, be egotistical, and care only for ourselves to the detriment of society and even to the detriment of our own humanity. These are very real possibilities in peacebuilding, even if unintended.

The purpose of this book is to help peacebuilders be attentive to the moral values and ethics involved in our work in order to contribute to good and right consciously; to contribute to our collective humanity, to flourishing, and to *being* good peacebuilders who do things right; to enable us to better talk about the issues that really matter, as the first vignette names. Thinking ethically in the midst of "wicked problems" requires skills, capacities, practice, and support. In this final chapter, I revisit the challenges that confront us as well as the reflection-action cycle and conclude by offering building blocks for more ethical peacebuilding practice.

REVIEWING THE CHALLENGES FOR ETHICAL THINKING AND ACTION

The challenges and barriers that inhibit ethical thinking in the field involve our individual skills and capacities as well as our work environments and the larger conflict and peacebuilding contexts in which we operate. These interconnect and include the following elements that individual peacebuilders often experience and that we therefore need to address in order to become more ethical in practice:

- Time pressures;
- Focus (e.g. avoid running down rabbit trails); and
- Trauma.

Together, these contribute pressures that encourage peacebuilders to rely on mental shortcuts, such as dogmatism, rationalization, and relativism, if and when thinking about moral problems. Mental shortcuts might help us operate expediently, but actually undercut ethical thinking and put us further behind in terms of thoughtful, well-timed responses that contribute positively in the long run.

Peacebuilders also face a set of challenges with respect to a general lack of attentiveness to moral values and ethical deliberation. This includes:

- Ignoring moral values;
- Ignoring differences in moral values and/or the different ways in which the same moral values are expressed;
- Homogenizing moral communities by assuming everyone holds the same values;
- Operating by a limited or overly narrow moral value frame;
- Reinforcing division or inequity in our moral value prioritization; and
- Mishandling moral value tensions.

This set of challenges around moral values relates to core moral considerations, which are at the heart of ethical thinking and action. In the field it means that peacebuilders tend to operate based on assumptions of what is good and right, which can compound problems and contribute harms.

Finally, there are a set of challenges that relate the ways in which we engage with others in discussions and decision-making in our peacebuilding work. This set of challenges includes:

- Tendencies toward conformity and obedience;
- Flawed group dynamics (i.e., groupthink, Abilene paradox, escalating commitment, concertive control, and moral exclusion); and
- Unethical work environments, including formal and informal norms, policies, and practices that operate in our workplaces.

Work environments, policies, and procedures can reinforce unethical or ethical messages and practices and unintentionally undermine well-designed and conceptualized peacebuilding.

These three sets of cumulative challenges are depicted in table 7.1. Addressing these challenges requires a mix of attentiveness, inquiry, dialogue, and engagement.

Table 7.1. Three Sets of Ethical Thinking Challenges

Individual Perception	*Moral Inattentiveness*	*Group Pressures*
• Limited time • Narrow focus • Trauma	• Mental shortcuts • Ignore moral values • Ignore difference • Ignore moral tensions • Homogenize • Limit moral values • Reinforce inequity and injustice in moral value prioritization	• Conformity • Obedience • Flawed group dynamics and/or decision-making (groupthink, Abilene paradox, escalating commitment, concertive control, moral exclusion) • Unethical work environments

CONFRONTING WICKED PROBLEMS IN PEACEBUILDING

The term "wicked problems" was coined in reference to urban planning challenges. It refers to large, complex problems that involve many stakeholders, interlocking components and systems, and many uncertainties. Other terms used to refer to these problems are "social messes" or "systems of systems." Because of the messiness, it is difficult to determine where to enter into a problem, how to respond, and what to change. Each wicked problem is understood to be unique. The advice to people working on wicked problems is to look to improve things and not to solve the problem. In 1973, Horst Rittel and Melvin Webber noted that wicked problems are not solved but "re-solved" as the problems and actors involved in the problems change over time; a dynamic, ongoing resolution process is required to continually respond to these evolving problems.

Peacebuilding as a whole presents itself as a wicked problem in this original meaning. Peacebuilding problems are complex, involve many stakeholders, interlocking components, systems, and uncertainties. Each endeavor is unique, and the actors and problems morph over time. A number of peacebuilding scholar–practitioners, such as Rob Ricigliano, John Paul Lederach, and Chip Hauss, draw on complexity theory and systems thinking in order to explore this aspect of peacebuilding and reframe how we think about the ends we seek in and through peacebuilding vis-à-vis complexity.[2]

It is intriguing that the term "wicked" is used in the context of complex problems. Rittel and Webber, who originally used the term in relation to public policy and urban planning, suggest "wicked" because it connotes malignant, vicious, tricky, and aggressive problems. They clearly state they do not refer to malicious intent, and so are not trying to suggest wicked problems are evil or morally wrong. Rittel and Webber do, however, suggest that it is morally objectionable if someone does not identify and respond to a wicked problem as such. That means if an expert in the field approaches a problem as if it was tame or simple, then he or she is morally irresponsible. The intervener is shirking his or her duty and making preventable mistakes that will not achieve the intended outcomes—in consequentialist language, the ends achieved will not be as good as any other course of action. Applying Rittel and Webber's moral injunction to peacebuilding means that addressing the full complexity inherent in peacebuilding becomes part of our moral responsibility. This is in line with what peacebuilding scholars like Ricigiliano, Lederach, and Hauss suggest as well.

Yet our moral decisions are not finished when we embrace complexity. Moral values are everywhere, and many of our practical decisions about interventions are informed by our beliefs about what is good and right. We are guided by our moral values with respect to the good we think we can do, who we are and how we act, the values we live out, the choices we make in terms of the framing of the problems we are addressing in and through peacebuilding, and the ends we look to achieve. As with wicked problems, we also need to continually be aware of and respond to the multidimensional nature of the unique challenges before us. We require a dynamic, ongoing process to assess and respond to the problems we see in the midst of complexity, and this *necessarily* includes reflection on our moral values in the midst of our complex, value-infused peacebuilding work.

The reflection-action cycle (discussed in chapter 2) is intended to help practitioners to do just that: to establish a dynamic system that helps us deliberate, decide, and act better together. The cycle is a conceptual tool to help think about when and where we can step back from the busy-ness of our work and create space for doable ethical reflection. What this cycle looks like in practice will vary, taking into consideration our work environment and our ability to analyze aspects of our work at a given moment in time. Yet, some version of a regular reflection-action cycle that deliberately engages ethical questions will help respond to complexity and nourish an ethical work environment (see chapter 6). The cycle will need to move in terms of the content being addressed in order to be responsive to the context, and yet it will repeat itself over time, as figure 7.1 is intended to depict, as part of attentive practice. The contents of what is explored in the reflection-action cycle are at the heart of this book. This is the content covered in chapters 2 through 6.

DOING GOOD WELL

We engage in and with communities that hold moral values that can be named in peacebuilding. We act as individuals and groups in locations affected by

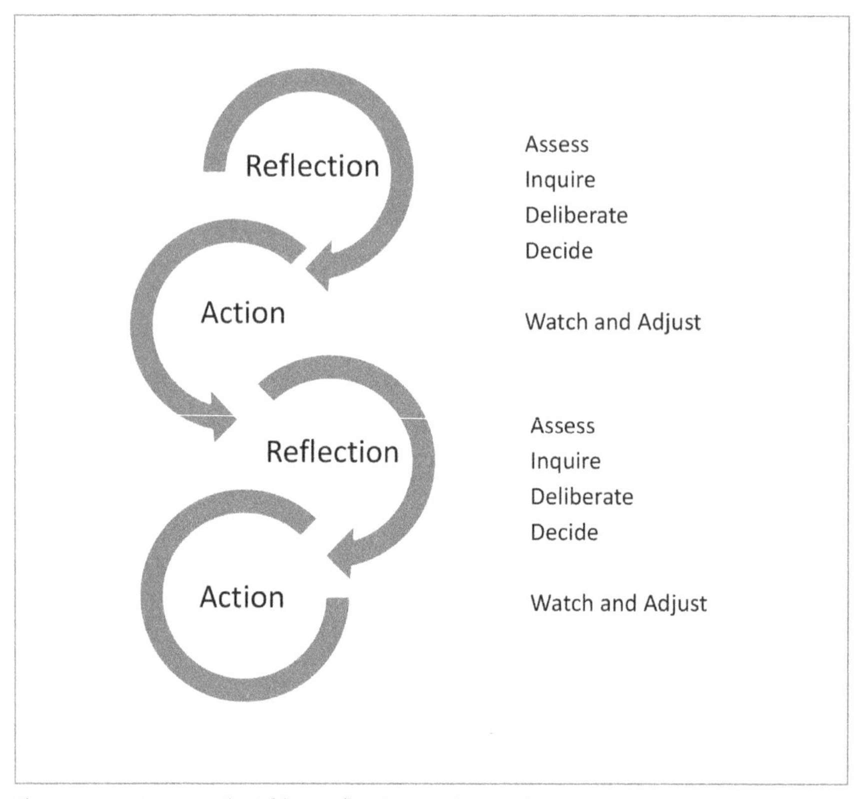

Figure 7.1. A Dynamic Ethics Reflection-Action Cycle

power dynamics, social identity, and the long shadow of conflict, which is shaped by and shapes our moral values. In order to engage in better, more ethical practice we need to improve how we think about moral values and their application. This means ethical thinking and it involves open and careful deliberation on moral values in dialogue with and response to others in the midst of busy and challenging work environments. The image in figure 7.2 aims to visually connect all of the pieces involved in thinking ethically together.

Moral values are at the heart of our judgments about what is right and wrong, good or bad. Moral values are infused in our technical language for peacebuilding as well as our thinking about why peacebuilding is important. Better ethical practice therefore begins with moral values: identifying them, analyzing them, questioning them, discussing them, and making decisions based upon them after careful inquiry and deliberation. How to begin doing this is the focus of chapter 3.

Figure 7.2. Ethical Thinking: Putting It All Together

Moral theories (explored in chapter 4) offer scaffolding to help consider problems and decisions from multiple moral value vantage points. Thinking about virtues, duties, relationships (care and Ubuntu), and the consequences of our actions are important aspects to consider in choosing an ethical course of action. The theories help us think about ourselves as peacebuilders and the virtues we embody, the relational networks in which we and our peace work are enmeshed and to which we respond, the intended and unintended consequences of our actions, and the obligations or duties that we want to see consistently upheld. The moral theories can help ensure we are not ignoring important moral value considerations that might matter to moral communities with whom we work. That said, there are other moral perspectives that can enrich thinking about ethics that may be particularly salient and important within a given context, and so the moral theories are suggestive rather than conclusive.

Creative problem-solving (chapter 5) is useful when moral values conflict. When we find ourselves confronting a tension between moral values, or appear to be on the horns of a dilemma, creativity can help us generate responses in order to meet multiple values in previously unimagined ways. Even so, the outcomes of our decisions may not meet all of our values, and it is important to identify and address these shortcomings in creative ways.

Ethical practice is clearly not about justifying our choices nor raising an accusing finger at colleagues and denouncing them with statements like "you are wrong!" Indeed, in the example of the staff responding to the vehicle accident (chapter 6), if a single-sided and accusatory approach was taken, then the senior managers' reception to considering differing moral value perspectives would have been negative. When we engage in moral value considerations, being respectful and listening to multiple sides of the issues can go a long way to opening up conversation. Further, being forthright and action-oriented in terms of identifying multiple possible responses and making concrete recommendations also facilitates engagement and action.

Ethical thinking necessitates peering into difficult decisions and accepting that we may have done wrong, or that we may be continuing to do wrong and that we can change. It involves looking into needs and problems deeply, openly, and carefully. It involves being willing to change our morally problematic behavior and initiatives as individuals as well as within teams and organizations. At times, it requires moral courage, so that people do not silence themselves in the face of harms and ethical violations. Developing the practical wisdom (*phronesis*) to recognize what is morally salient or important takes time and can be enhanced through education and practice. The simulations in this book are intended to help do this, as are reflection discussions in a reflection-action cycle.

Our teams and organizations can enable or suppress open, ethical thinking and engagement and therefore also require attention. Peacebuilders, in consultation with stakeholders can do better at designing decision-making processes that include ethical discussions that move conversations about ethics forward in ways that validate questions and avoid premature or false agreement. The PBI example (see chapter 2) modeled this by allowing for context-based decisions and personal choice even after coming to a working consensus on an overall principle of action. It is when we act that we exercise our moral agency, and we can monitor our ethical performance in action as part of our reflection cycle in case things go wrong despite our best thinking.

ROBUST ETHICAL ENGAGEMENT FOR PEACEBUILDING PRACTITIONERS

What does robust engagement on ethics look like in practice? We have some examples in the stories presented in earlier chapters: the examples of creative

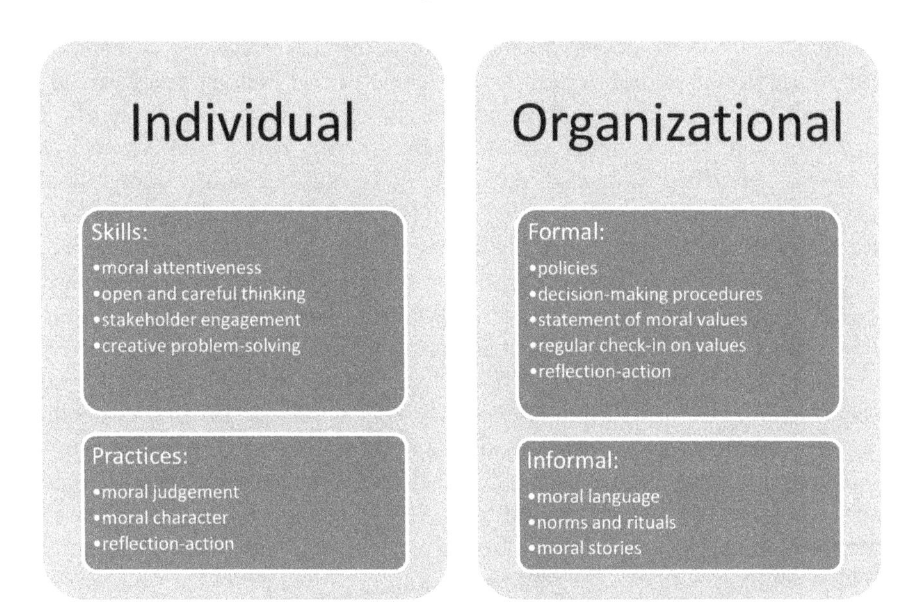

Figure 7.3. Building Blocks for Robust Ethical Engagement

thinking around competing moral values, healthy decision-making processes, valuing voices that identify moral problems, and being responsive. Building blocks for engaging with ethics robustly include developing our individual capacities to recognize moral values and to engage with them constructively in ethical deliberation with multiple stakeholders in conflict contexts. Another set of building blocks relate to institutional capacities and the formal and informal structures and procedures that support ethical engagement. This ranges from organizational vision statements to policies and decision-making practices on the formal side, to the informal stories, language, and rituals that are enacted as part of the work environment. The image in figure 7.3 maps out these basic elements. This is an area, however, that requires further thinking, practical experimentation, research, and development in peacebuilding.

AMBITIOUS AIMS AND EVERYDAY PRACTICES

At the start of this book, I reframed Hannah Arendt's observation of Eichmann for peacebuilders. I wrote: "The sad truth of the matter is that most of the harms done in and through peacebuilding are done by people with good intentions who did not think too deeply about good or bad in their everyday work." It is fitting to return to this challenge to conclude.

Arendt's observation that Eichmann demonstrated a curious inability to think, particularly in moral terms, was insightful for helping people to understand that horrendous wrongs and evil *do not* always occur because of malicious intent.[3] Eichmann was doing his job and being efficient at it as a German SS officer during World War II. He did not think deeply about the people on the receiving end of his efficiently organized transportation to death camps. He was not malicious, yet the effects of his actions were horrific. Eichmann presents us with a warning of the possible dangers and outcomes that can occur when not thinking in moral terms, when we only think about our jobs without contemplating the moral value dimensions of our work. His is an extreme case in that the Nazi structures formalized and supported tremendously immoral behavior, and so we need to be careful with this example in order to not draw too many parallels. Nevertheless, it raises the specter of horrendous wrongs in the absence of attention—individual and organizational—to moral questions. It reminds us that moral values in the midst of conflict and war are frequently inverted, subverted, or ignored. It also reminds us that large groups of people are often excluded from moral consideration in the midst of war and conflict.

The challenge for those engaged in peacebuilding work is to ensure our work responds to the ethical problems we face. For the most part, we do not face dramatic moral choices, but lower levels of decisions: to travel to an insecure area? To provide aid to those who appear to be former combatants? How broadly to share information? Where to sit during a community meeting? We make small choices that circumscribe and foreclose a future set of choices. To make good decisions or better decisions, we can foster and sustain our ability to think and ask questions in order to recognize and avoid harms and moral pitfalls. Our challenge is to *think* even while we *do* peacebuilding. Doing good well requires work. It requires skills. It requires practice. It requires an enabling environment. And, drawing on the moral values explored in this book, it involves treating people as ends, living out virtues, caring for others, avoiding harms, contributing to good ends, and helping constitute collective flourishing and a greater humanity. These, like peacebuilding itself, are ambitious aims *and* everyday practices.

FOR FURTHER EXPLORATION

Here are some questions and activities that you can use to further think about issues raised in this chapter:

- Interview one person and find out about her or his ethical high moments. What happened? What did she or he do? What made the response ethical? When the interview is complete, switch roles and have the interviewer become the interviewee. When the second interview is done, look over the two responses to see if there are patterns: What can we learn from our own ethical high moments?
- What skills do you think you need to foster more ethical peacebuilding? What is needed in your organization or community to foster more ethical peacebuilding?
- What inhibits your ability to be ethical in your work environment? What needs to change in order to create space for ethical deliberation?

NOTES

1. The opening vignettes come from male and female colleagues working in nongovernmental organizations as well as international organizations, some working in their country of origin and others working internationally.

2. The discussion of wicked problems draws from Horst W. J. Rittel and Melvin M. Webber's original journal article titled "Dilemmas in a General Theory of Planning" (*Policy Sciences,* 4:155–69; 1973). For further exploration of complexity and systems approaches to peacebuilding, see Rob Ricigliano's *Making Peace Last: A Toolbox for Sustainable Peacebuilding* (New York: Routledge, 2012), John Paul Lederach's *The Moral Imagination: The Art and Soul of Building Peace* (New York: Oxford University Press, 2005), or Charles (Chip) Hauss's *Security 2.0: Dealing with Global Wicked Problems* (Lanham, MD: Rowman & Littlefield, 2016).

3. Hannah Arendt's reference to Eichmann comes from the lecture "Thinking and Moral Considerations" (*Social Research*, 38(3):417–46, 1971). Arendt explores the effects of bureaucratization on moral thinking more extensively in her book *Eichmann in Jerusalem: A Report on the Banality of Evil* (New York: Penguin Classics, 2006).

Bibliography

Action Aid, Afghanaid, Care Afghanistan, Christian Aid, Concern Worldwide, Norwegian Refugee Council, Oxfam International, and Trocaire. (2010). Quick Impact, Quick Collapse: The Dangers of Militarized Aid in Afghanistan. United Kingdom.

Anderson, M. B. (1999). *Do No Harm: Supporting Capacities for Peace through Aid.* Boulder, CO: Lynne Reinner Publishers.

Anderson, M. B., and Olson, L. (2003). *Confronting War: Critical Lessons for Peace Practitioners.* Cambridge, MA: Collaborative for Development Action, Inc., Reflecting on Peace Practice Project.

Arendt, H. (1971). "Thinking and Moral Considerations: A Lecture." *Social Research,* 38 (3): 417–46.

———. (2006). *Eichmann in Jerusalem: A Report on the Banality of Evil.* New York: Penguin Classics.

Aristotle. (2002). *Nichomachean Ethics.* Translated by Christopher Rowe and Sarah Broadie. New York: Oxford University Press.

Association for Conflict Resolution. (2010). "ACR Ethical Principles: Final Report of ACR Ethics Committee," from http://www.acrnet.org/Page.aspx?id=1960.

Autesserre, S. (2009). "Hobbes and the Congo: Frames, Local Violence, and International Intervention." *International Organization,* 63: 249–80.

———. (2014). *Peaceland: Conflict Resolution and the Everyday Politics of International Intervention.* New York: Cambridge University Press.

Barakat, S. (2006). Mid-term Evaluation Report of the National Solidarity Programme (NSP), Afghanistan. York, United Kingdom: Post-war Reconstruction & Development Unit (PRDU), The University of York; and Ministry of Rural Rehabilitation and Development, Islamic Republic of Afghanistan.

Barker, J. (1993). "Tightening the Iron Cage: Concertive Control in Self-Managing Teams." *Administrative Sciences Quarterly,* 38: 408–37.

Beath, A., Christia, F., and Enikolopov, R. (2015). "The National Solidarity Program: Assessing the Effects of Community-Driven Development in Afghanistan; Policy

Research Working Paper 7415." Washington, DC: World Bank Group; Office of the Chief Economist, East Asia, and the Pacific Region.
Bellamy, A., and Williams, P. D. (2010). *Understanding Peacekeeping*. Second edition. Malden, MA: Polity Press.
Bennett, J., Alexander, J., Saltmarshe, D., Phillipson, R., and Marsden, P. (2009). Country Programme Evaluation Afghanistan. *Evaluation Report EV 696*. United Kingdom: Department for International Development (DFID).
Boesen, I. W. (2004). From Subjects to Citizens: Local Participation in the National Solidarity Programme. Kabul: Afghanistan Research and Evaluation Unit (AREA).
Boulding, E. (1990). *Building a Global Civic Culture: Education for an Interdependent World*. Syracuse, NY: Syracuse University Press.
Boutros-Ghali, B. (1992). A/47/277–S/24111. *An Agenda for Peace: Preventive Diplomacy, Peacemaking and Peace-keeping*. New York: United Nations.
Call, C. T., and Wyeth, V., eds. (2008). *Building States to Build Peace*. Boulder, CO: Lynne Rienner Publishers, Inc.
Campbell, S., Chandler, D., and Sabaratnam, M., eds. (2011). *A Liberal Peace? The Problems and Practices of Peacebuilding*. New York: Zed Books.
Clarke, H., ed. (2009). *People Power: Unarmed Resistance and Global Solidarity*. London: Pluto Press.
Cohen, C. (2001). *Working with Integrity: A Guidebook for Peacebuilders Asking Ethical Questions*. Waltham, MA: The Brandeis Initiative in Intercommunal Coexistence, a program of the International Center for Ethics, Justice and Public Life, Brandeis University.
Corcoran, C. T., Bellegarde, D., and Prentice, J. (1994). The Young Chippewayan Inquiry into the Claim Regarding Stoney Knoll Indian Reserve No. 107. Ottawa, ON: Indian Claims Commission.
Coy, P. G. (2001). "Shared Risks and Research Dilemmas on a Peace Brigades International Team in Sri Lanka." *Journal of Contemporary Ethnography*, 30: 575–606.
———. (2003). "Negotiating Identity and Danger under the Gun: Consensus Decision Making on Peace Brigades International Teams." *Consensus Decision Making, Northern Ireland and Indigenous Movements*, 24: 85–122.
da Costa Babo Soares, D. (2003). "Branching from the Trunk: East Timorese Perceptions of Nationalism in Transition." PhD dissertation. Department of Anthropology, Australia National University.
Davis, D. B. (2006). *Inhuman Bondage: The Rise and Fall of Slavery in the New World*. New York: Oxford University Press.
Davis, M. (2005). "The Moral Justifiability of Torture and other Cruel, Inhuman, or Degrading Treatment." *International Journal of Applied Philosophy* 19, no. 2: 161–78.
De La Torre, M. A. (2013). "Introduction." In *Ethics: A Liberative Approach*, edited by Miguel A. De la Torre, 1–6. Minneapolis: Fortress Press.
Deutsch, M. (1990). "Psychological Roots of Moral Exclusion." *Journal of Social Issues*, 46 (1): 21–25. doi: 10.1111/j.1540–4560.1990.tb00269.x.
Doell, L. (1977). *History of the Mennonites and Natives in the Last One Hundred Years*. Saskatoon: Native Ministries, Mennonite Central Committee Canada.

Douglass, F. (2005). *Fredrick Douglass' Narrative of the Life of Frederick Douglass, an American Slave*. New York: Signet Books.

Fast, L. A., Neufeldt, R. C., and Schirch, L. (2002). "Toward Ethically Grounded Conflict Interventions: Reevaluating Challenges in the 21st Century." *International Negotiation*, 7 (2): 185–207.

Fisher, R., and Ury, W. (1991). *Getting to Yes: Negotiating Agreement without Giving In*. New York: Penguin Books.

Fisher, R., Ury, W., and Patton, B. (2011). *Getting to Yes: Negotiating Agreement Without Giving In*. Third edition. New York: Penguin Books.

Fisher, R., ed. (2005). *Paving the Way: Contributions of Interactive Conflict Resolution to Peacemaking*. Lanham, MD: Lexington Books.

Fishstein, P., and Wilder, A. (2012). *Winning Hearts and Minds? Examining the Relationship between Aid and Security in Afghanistan*. Medford, MA: Feinstein International Center.

Fournier, D. M. (2005). "Evaluation." In *Encyclopedia of Evaluation*, edited by Sandra Mathison, 140–41. Thousand Oaks, CA: Sage Publications, Inc.

French, J. R. P., and Raven, B. (1959). "The Bases of Power." In *Studies in Social Power*, edited by D. Cartwright, 150–67. Ann Arbor, MI: University of Michigan, Institute for Social Research.

Gabbatt, A. (2014). "'Not All Spying is Bad': Snowden Calls for Whistleblower Protection in Q&A." *The Guardian*, Jan. 23, 2014. Online edition, from http://www.theguardian.com/world/2014/jan/23/edward-snowden-nsa-whistleblower-courage-foundation.

Galtung, J. (1976). "Three Approaches to Peace: Peacekeeping, Peacemaking and Peacebuilding." In *Peace, War and Defense: Essays in Peace Research, Volume Two*, edited by Johan Galtung, 282–304. Copenhagen: Christian Ejlers and PRIO.

Gilligan, C. (1982). *In a Different Voice: Psychological Theory and Women's Development*. Cambridge, MA: Harvard University Press.

Gopin, M. (2012). *Bridges Across an Impossible Divide: the Inner Lives of Arab and Jewish Peacemakers*. New York: Oxford University Press.

Greenwald, G., MacAskill, E., and Poitras, L. (2013). "Edward Snowden: The Whistleblower Behind the NSA Surveillance Revelations." *Guardian*. Online edition, from http://www.theguardian.com/world/2013/jun/09/edward-snowden-nsa-whistleblower-surveillance.

Grimk, A. E. (2000). "Appeal to the Christian Women of the South." In *Walden and Civil Disobedience*, edited by Paul Lauter, 267–86. New York: Houghton Mifflin Company.

Hauss, C. (2016). *Security 2.0: Dealing with Global Wicked Problems*. Lanham, MD: Rowman & Littlefield.

Headley, W. R., and Neufeldt, R. C. (2010). "Catholic Relief Services: Catholic Peacebuilding in Practice." In *Peacebuilding: Catholic Theology, Ethics and Praxis*, edited by Robert J. Schreiter, R. Scott Appleby, and Gerard F. Powers, 125–154. Maryknoll, NY: Orbis Books.

Held, V. (2006). "The Ethics of Care." In *The Oxford Handbook of Ethical Theory*, edited by David Copp. 537–66. New York: Oxford University Press.

Higashi, D. (2008). "The Challenge of Constructing Legitimacy in Peacebuilding: Case of Afghanistan." CIR Working Paper No. 47. Vancouver, British Colombia: Centre of International Relations.

Hutchings, K. (2010). *Global Ethics: An Introduction*. Malden, MA: Polity Press.

International Alert. (1998). *Code of Conduct: Conflict Transformation Work*. London, UK: International Alert.

International Crisis Group. (2006). "Resolving Timor-Leste's Crisis." Jakarta/Brussels: International Crisis Group.

International Organization for Migration. (Sept. 6, 2005). "Afghanistan: IOM's Quick Impact Projects Program Receives US$32 Million of Additional Funding." International Organization for Migration.

Irvin Painter, N. (1997). *Sojourner Truth, A Life, A Symbol*. New York: W. W. Norton.

Janis, I. L. (1982/1972). *Groupthink: Psychological Studies of Policy Decisions and Fiascoes*. Boston, MA: Houghton Mifflin Company.

Jarstad, A. K. (2008). "Dilemmas of war-to-democracy transitions: theories and concepts." In *From War to Democracy: Dilemmas of Peacebuilding*, edited by Anna K. Jarstad and Timothy D. Sisk, 17–36. New York: Cambridge University Press.

Johnson, C. (2007). *Ethics in the Workplace: Tools and Tactics for Organizational Transformation*. Thousand Oaks, CA: Sage Publications, Inc.

Kelman, H. C., and Cohen, S. P. (1976). "The Problem-Solving Workshop: A Social-Psychological Contribution to the Resolution of International Conflicts." *Journal of Peace Research*, 13 (2): 79–90.

Kelman, H. C., and Warwick, D. P. (1978). "The Ethics of Social Intervention: Goals, Means, and Consequences." In *The Ethics of Social Intervention*, edited by Gordon Bermant, Herbert C. Kelman, and Donald P. Warwick, 3–33. Washington, DC: Hemisphere Publishing Corporation.

Kidder, R. M. (2005). *Moral Courage*. New York: Harper Collins.

Kohrs Campbell, K., Huxman, S. S., and Burkholder, T., eds. (2014). *The Rhetorical Act: Thinking, Speaking and Writing Critically*. Fifth edition. Stamford, CT: Cengage Learning.

Laue, J., and Cormick, G. (1978). "The Ethics of Intervention in Community Disputes." In *Ethics of Social Intervention*, edited by Gordon Bermant, Herbert C. Kelman, and Donald P. Warwick, 205–32. Washington, DC: Hemisphere Publishing Corporation.

Leach, M. (2007). "History Teaching: Challenges and Alternatives." In *East Timor: Beyond Independence*, edited by Damien Kingsbury and Michael Leach, 193–207. Victoria: Monash University Press.

Lederach, J. P. (1997). *Building Peace: Sustainable Reconciliation in Divided Societies*. Washington, DC: United States Institute of Peace.

———. (2005). *The Moral Imagination: The Art and Soul of Building Peace*. New York: Oxford University Press.

Lederach, J. P., Neufeldt, R., and Culbertson, H. (2007). *Reflective Peacebuilding: A Planning, Monitoring and Learning Toolkit*. Mindanao, PH: The Joan B. Kroc Institute for International Peace Studies and Catholic Relief Services, SEAPRO.

Mac Ginty, R., ed. (2013). *Routledge Handbook of Peacebuilding*. New York: Routledge.

MacIntyre, A. (1981). *After Virtue: A Study in Moral Theory*. Notre Dame, IN: University of Notre Dame Press.

Mackie, J. L. (1978). "Can There be a Right-based Moral Theory?" *Midwest Studies in Philosophy*, 3 (1): 350–59. doi: 10.1111/j.1475–4975.1978.tb00366.x.

Mathewes, C. (2010). *Understanding Religious Ethics*. West Sussex: Wiley-Blackwell.

McCarthy, T. (2015). "Edward Snowden: Clinton Made 'False Claim' about Whistleblower Protection." *Guardian*, Oct. 16, 2015. Online edition, from http://www.theguardian.com/us-news/2015/oct/16/edward-snowden-hillary-clinton-false-claim-whistleblower-protection.

Michalko, M. (2001). *Cracking Creativity: The Secrets of Creative Genius*. Berkley, CA: Ten Speed Press.

Milgram, S. (1963). "Behavioral Study of Obedience." *The Journal of Abnormal and Social Psychology*, 67 (4): 371–78.

———. (1974). *Obedience to Authority: An Experimental View*. New York: Harper & Row.

Monsutti, A. (2012). "Fuzzy Sovereignty: Rural Reconstruction in Afghanistan, between Democracy Promotion and Power Games." *Comparative Studies in Society and History*, 54 (3): 563–91.

Morris, S., Stephenson, J. (S.), Ciminelli, P., Muncy, D., Wilson, T., and Nugent, A. (2006). "Provincial Reconstruction Teams in Afghanistan: An Interagency Assessment." Washington, DC: Department of State, Office of the Coordinator for Stabilization and Reconstruction; Department of Defense, Joint Center for Operational Analysis/U.S. Joint Forces Command; and U.S. Agency for International Development, Bureau for Policy and Program Coordination.

Murithi, T. (2009). *The Ethics of Peacebuilding*. Edinburgh: Edinburgh University Press Ltd.

Murove, M. F., ed. (2009). *African Ethics: An Anthology of Comparative and Applied Ethics*. Scottsville, South Africa: University of KwaZulu-Natal Press.

Nemeth, C. (1997). "Managing Innovation: When Less Is More." *California Management Review*, 40 (1): 59–74.

Neufeldt, R. C. (2005). "Barn Razing: Change and Continuity in Identity during Conflict." PhD Doctoral dissertation, School of International Service, American University.

Neufeldt, R. C. (2014). "Doing Good Better: Expanding the Ethics of Peacebuilding." *International Peacekeeping*, 21 (4): 427–42.

Neusner, J., and Chilton, B., eds. (2009). *The Golden Rule: The Ethics of Reciprocity in World Religions*. New York: Continuum International Publishing Group.

Ngcoya, M. (2015). "Ubuntu: Toward an Emancipatory Cosmopolitanism?" *International Political Sociology*, 9 (3): 248–62. doi: 10.1111/ips.12095.

Nicolson, R., ed. (2008). *Persons in Community: African Ethics in a Global Culture*. Scottsville, South Africa: University of KwaZulu-Natal Press.

Niebuhr, H. R. (1963). *The Responsible Self: An Essay in Christian Moral Philosophy*. New York: Harper & Row.

Niner, S. (2007). "Martyrs, Heroes and Warriors: The Leadership of East Timor." In *East Timor: Beyond Independence,* edited by Damien Kingsbury and Michael Leach, 113–28. Victoria: Monash University Press.

Olfert, E. (2006). "A Historic Meeting on Stoney Knoll." *Intotemak*, 35 (3): 1, 4.

Opotow, S. (1990a). "Deterring Moral Exclusion." *Journal of Social Issues,* 46 (1): 173–82. doi: 10.1111/j.1540–4560.1990.tb00280.x.

———. (1990b). "Moral Exclusion and Injustice: An Introduction." *Journal of Social Issues,* 46 (1): 1–20. doi: 10.1111/j.1540–4560.1990.tb00268.x.

Paris, R. (2002). "International Peacebuilding and the 'Mission Civilisatrice.'" *Review of International Studies,* 28 (4): 637–56.

Patton, M. Q. 2008. *Utilization Focused Evaluation*. Fourth edition. Thousand Oaks, CA: Sage Publications, Inc.

Ponzio R. J. (2011). *Democratic Peacebuilding: Aiding Afghanistan and Other Fragile States*. New York: Oxford University Press.

Rawls, J. (1971). *A Theory of Justice*. Cambridge, MA: Harvard University Press.

Riciglino, R. (2012). *Making Peace Last: A Toolbox for Sustainable Peacebuilding.* New York: Routledge.

Rittel, H. W. J., and Webber, M. M. (1973). "Dilemmas in a General Theory of Planning." *Policy Sciences,* 4: 155–69.

Rorty, R. (1996). "Who are We? Moral Universalism and Economic Triage." *Diogenes,* 173 (44): 5–15.

Schön, D. A. (1983). *The Reflective Practitioner: How Professionals Think in Action.* New York: Basic Books, Inc.

Shaw, R. (2005). "Rethinking Truth and Reconciliation Commissions: Lessons from Sierra Leone." Washington, DC: United States Institute of Peace.

Slim, H. (2001). "Dealing with Moral Dilemmas." In *Peacebuilding: A Field Guide*, edited by Luc Reychler and Thania Paffenholz, 497–509. Boulder, CO: Lynne Rienner Publishers, Inc.

Staw, B. M. (1976). "Knee-Deep in the Big Muddy: A Study of Escalating Commitment to a Chosen Course of Action." *Organizational Behavior and Human Performance,* 16 (1): 27–44.

Sterba, J. P. (2005). *The Triumph of Practice over Theory in Ethics*. New York: Oxford University Press.

Tarnoff, C. (2012). Afghanistan: U.S. Foreign Assistance. Washington, DC: Congressional Research Service.

Thiessen, C. (2014). *Local Ownership of Peacebuilding in Afghanistan.* Lanham, MD: Lexington Books.

Timmons, M. (2010). *Disputed Moral Issues: A Reader*. New York: Oxford University Press.

Tutu, D. (1999). *No Future without Forgiveness*. New York: Doubleday.

United Nations Security Council. (2001). Security Council Resolution 1386. New York, NY: United Nations.

Uvin, P. (1998). *Aiding Violence: The Development Enterprise in Rwanda.* West Hartford, CT: Kumarian Press.

Ward, M. (2009). "Quick Impact Projects Slow Progress in Afghanistan." *The Boston Globe*, October 15, op-ed. Online edition, from www.boston.com/bostonglobe/editorial_opinion/oped/articles/2009/10/15/quick_impact_projects_slow_progress_in_afghanistan/.

Warfield, W. (2002). "Is It the Right Thing to Do? A Practical Framework for Ethical Decisions." In *A Handbook of International Peacebuilding: Into the Eye of the Storm*, edited by John Paul Lederach and Janice Moomaw Jenner, 213–23. San Francisco, CA: Jossey-Bass.

Weston, A. (2013). *A 21st Century Ethical Toolbox*. Third edition. New York: Oxford University Press.

———. (2007). *Creative Problem-Solving in Ethics*. New York: Oxford University Press.

———. (2011). *A Practical Companion to Ethics*. Fourth edition. New York: Oxford University Press.

Whitmore, T. D. (2010). "'If They Kill Us at Least the Others Will Have More Time to Get Away': The Ethics of Risk in Ethnographic Practice." *Practical Matters*, 3: 1–28.

Zimbardo, P. G., Haney, C., and Banks, C. (1973). "The Mind Is a Formidable Jailer: A Pirandellian Prison." *New York Times Magazine*, April 8, Section 6: 38–60.

Index of Terms

About the Author

Reina Neufeldt is an assistant professor in Peace and Conflict Studies at Conrad Grebel University College, University of Waterloo. Previously she was an assistant professor at the School of International Service, American University, and a visiting research fellow at the Kroc Institute for International Peace Studies, University of Notre Dame. She holds an MA in social psychology (York University) and a PhD in international relations (American University). For numerous years Dr. Neufeldt worked as a peacebuilding technical advisor for Catholic Relief Services based in Baltimore as well as in Southeast Asia. In addition, she has worked with various non-governmental organizations in the areas of monitoring, evaluation, and reflective learning. Dr. Neufeldt coauthored *Reflective Peacebuilding: A Planning, Monitoring and Learning Toolkit* and *Peacebuilding: A Caritas Manual.* Her articles have appeared in *International Peacekeeping*, *Nations and Nationalism*, *International Negotiation*, *Journal of Peacebuilding and Development*, and *Peace and Change.*

CPSIA information can be obtained
at www.ICGtesting.com
Printed in the USA
BVHW051742140822
644567BV00005B/109

9 781442 264922